כל המאריך באחד תר"ץ

ONENESS
IN CREATION

כל המאריך באחד תר"ץ

ONENESS
IN CREATION

a chasidic discourse by
Rabbi Yosef Yitzchak Schneersohn
זצוקללה"ה נבג"מ זי"ע
of Lubavitch

•

translation by
Rabbi Y. Eliezer Danzinger

annotation and commentary by
Rabbi Avraham D. Vaisfiche
Rabbi Ari Sollish

KEHOT PUBLICATION SOCIETY
770 Eastern Parkway / Brooklyn, New York 11213

ONENESS IN CREATION

Published and Copyrighted © 2004
Second Printing 2007
by
KEHOT PUBLICATION SOCIETY
770 Eastern Parkway / Brooklyn, New York 11213
(718) 774-4000 / Fax (718) 774-2718

Orders:
291 Kingston Avenue / Brooklyn, New York 11213
(718) 778-0226 / Fax (718) 778-4148
www.kehotonline.com

ISBN: 978-0-8266-0739-3

Manufactured in the United States of America

CONTENTS

PREFACE

We are pleased to present *Oneness in Creation*, as part of the much acclaimed Chasidic Heritage Series.

In 5689 (1929), Rabbi Yosef Yitzchak Schneersohn, the sixth Lubavitcher Rebbe, of blessed memory, who was then based in Riga, Latvia, visited the United States of America. He spent ten months on American soil, traveling from New York to as far west as S. Louis, stopping along the way at cities with large Jewish populations.

One of these cities was Chicago. Rabbi Yosef Yitzchak held Chicago dear, as it was home to quite a large number of Chabad-Lubavitch Chasidim. It was here, in the spring of 5690 (1930), that the present discourse, beginning with the Hebrew words *Kol Hamaarich B'Echad*, was originally delivered.[1]

* * *

Oneness in Creation examines the most fundamental of prayers—the twice-daily recited *Shema*. In the *Shema*, we proclaim *Havaya Echad*—"G-d is One." G-d's Oneness, Rabbi Yosef Yitzchak explains in the discourse, is not a transcendent Singularity, separate and distinct from creation, but an immanent Harmony with all of existence. G-d is One with creation, with nature, with every living being, because G-dliness is the true life-force of everything. All of existence, at its core, is but a unique manifestation of Divinity.

Knowing this, Rabbi Yosef Yitzchak says, one will recognize that ultimately it is G-d Who charts the course of man's life and Who provides man's sustenance. One will then view his pursuit of a livelihood in an entirely new light, con-

---

1. The discourse was originally published in Hebrew in honor of 12-13 Tammuz 5690 (1930), Rabbi Yosef Yitzchak's birthday and the anniversary of his release from Soviet imprisonment. It was subsequently published in *Sefer Hamaamarim Kuntresim*, vol. 1, p. 102a ff.

ducting his business affairs in consonance with Torah's high standards.

This, continues Rabbi Yosef Yitzchak, is the purpose of the soul's descent into the physical world: to reveal G-d's quintessential Oneness in all of creation, by learning Torah, fulfilling the *mitzvot*, and conducting one's material pursuits in the proper manner. This is a task incumbent upon every person, no matter where he may be. Hence, the word *Echad* is comprised of three letters: the *aleph* (the numerical value of one), symbolizing G-d; the *chet* (eight), signifying the soul's descent from on High down through the metaphysical seven heavens and into this world; and the *dalet* (four), indicating the soul's task to reveal G-d's Oneness throughout the four corners of the world.

* * *

As is the trademark of the Chasidic Heritage Series, *Oneness in Creation* is entirely reader-friendly, featuring a new, lucid translation of the text, as well as numerous explanatory notes and commentary. The original Hebrew text also appears on facing pages, newly typeset and vocalized.

To help the reader understand the unique significance of the discourse and of the Chicago visit, we have included: a) a brief historical sketch of Rabbi Yosef Yitzchak's delivery of the discourse, as an introduction; b) an open letter to the Jewish community of Chicago written by Rabbi Yosef Yitzchak, that originally appeared in the *Chicago Daily Jewish Courier* on May 9, 1930, in which Rabbi Yosef Yitzchak expresses his impressions of the visit, and blesses the entire community. The letter appears here as an appendix.

The discourse was translated by Rabbi Y. Eliezer Danzinger. Rabbis Avraham D. Vaisfiche and Ari Sollish added the annotation and commentary. Special thanks are due to Rabbis Dovid Olidort and Yosef B. Friedman for their editorial guidance.

Kehot Publication Society

Rosh Chodesh Sivan 5764

RABBI YOSEF YITZCHAK SCHNEERSOHN
זצוקללה"ה נבג"מ זי"ע
5640-5710 (1880-1950)
during his visit to Chicago, 5690 (1930)

בס"ד.

אסיפת אגודת חסידים אנשי חב"ד נ?כהכנ"ס ליובאוויטש.
מוצש"ק שמיני

כל המאריך באחד מאריכין לו ימיו ושנותיו/ ברכות י"ג ב'/ וצ"ל מחז"ע האריכות
באחד, ומחו אריכות ימים ושנים דמי שהוא מאריך באחד מאריכין לו
ימיו ושנותיו.א"ר אחא בר' יעקב ובד', אמר רב אשי ובלבד שלא

יחטוף כח', וצ"ל ... ושנותיו. דהנה תיבת אחד חוא נ' אותיות . א' ח' ד', והאריכות
הוא כחד' ובלבד שלא יחטוף גם את חח', וצ"ל מחו האריכות בחד' ואזחרתו של רב אשי
שלא יחטוף בחח', דמכל זה מובן דהאריכות בחד' הוא דוקא כשאינו חוטף את חח'.
והנה מאמר זה דכל המאריך באחד הוא חמשך חברייתא דתנו רבנן שמע ישראל חוי'
אלקינו חוי' אחד עד כאן צריכים כוונת חלב דברי ר' מאיר אמר רבא והלכה כר' מאיר.
וחנה ישנו כוונת חמוח וכוונת חלב , כוונת חמוח הוא חשגה שכלית מה שמיגע מוחו
לחכין ולחשיג ענין שכלי עד שיעמוד עליו ויכינו בכל פרטי ע ניניו, וכוונת חלב

ולחביא משבתו חמורח וחשנ ... במחכח אל חפועל כמדות סובות וחיינו
לחסיר כל מדה מנונת לעקרח ולשרש אשר כל תראה ... וכל חמצא ... שנד ... עליו חדבר
חלא מוב כין אם נ?אר דנר בין אדם למקום (כין אם נ?אר דנר בין אדם לחבירו) וכל
יגיעתו וחשתדלוחו חוא לנסוע בעצמן מדות סובות וחנהגות ישרות כין בדברים שבן
אדם למקום וכין בדברים שבן אדם לחבירו וחל"ע כוונת חלב לכוון את לבו. ולבא
פליג לכל שייפין לחביא כל מדה סובה לפועל ממש. אמירת שמע ישראל כו' אחד
ידיעת וחשנח אחדות חבורא ב"ח.כונ... שמע ישראל,שחישראל ישמע ויכין וישיג כי
חוי' אלקינו, דאלקינו כחינו וחיותנו הוא חוי'. דחנה שם אלקים חוא לשון כח
וכמ"ש ואת אילי חארץ לקח שמורה על חכח וחחזוק ולכן ואלקים בג'ימ' חסבע דבכל
דבר ודבר חרי סבעו הוא כחו . וחאנו אומרים חוי' אלקינו, ...
הוא חוי', מה שלמעלה :מן חסבע ... סבע הוא חמונדר בזמן ומקום, ... במקום
זה חוא מונבל כחגבלותיו , וכן חוא בזמן שמונבל כחגבלת דעבר חוח
ועתיד ,וחוי'חוא חי'חוה ויחי' כאחד שחוא למעלה מן חמקום ולמעלה מן חזמן.
וזחו חוי' אלקינו דחסבע ... כ?ונ ... ישראל חוא למעלח מחומן
... חחגבלות דזמן ומקום ...
וחנה ידיעת וחשנח דבר זח חוא בא ע"י חחחכונונות כחוי' אחד כי אחד פירושו חוא
... אלא שחאחדות ניכרת ... חחחכונונות כמש"ח ...
כח' אחד חנח ע"ז כאים לידי חכרה דחוי' אלקינ... וחיוחנו חוא חוי' וא"כ חרי

Facsimile of the original typed manuscript of *Kol Hamaarich B'echad*,
with handwritten notes by Rabbi Yosef Yitzchak Schneersohn

INTRODUCTION

INTRODUCTION
HISTORICAL SKETCH

Chicago, Nissan 5690 (1930).

The sixth Lubavitcher Rebbe, Rabbi Yosef Yitzchak Schneersohn, of righteous memory, had just completed an eleven-week visit to Chicago, during his ten-month stay in the United States. Having arrived in New York in Elul 5689 (1929), Rabbi Yosef Yitzchak's itinerary included visits to several major cities, among them Philadelphia, Milwaukee, Detroit, S. Louis and Boston.

The purpose of Rabbi Yosef Yitzchak's trip was two-fold: firstly, he wished to create public awareness about the dire situation of Russian Jewry at the time; secondly, he wished to bolster and encourage *Yiddishkeit* in America.[1]

Rabbi Yosef Yitzchak's itinerary also included a visit to Washington, where he was to be received by President Herbert Hoover in the White House. Here, he would thank the President for the religious freedom provided by the United States and for the government's interest in the well-being of Jewish communities abroad.

In those days, Chicago was home to a large number of Lubavitch Chasidim. The Chasidim established several Lubavitch *shuls*, including *Anshe Lubawitz, Beit Hakneset Tzemach Tzedek, Shaarei Tfila B'nai Reuven* and *Shaarei Tfila Nusach Ari*. These *shuls* hosted Rabbi Yosef Yitzchak's public gatherings, where hundreds and sometimes thousands of people streamed to hear his words of Torah and inspiration.

During his stay in Chicago, Rabbi Yosef Yitzchak delivered eleven Chasidic discourses. The *maamar* presented

---

1. See Rabbi Yosef Yitzchak's *Igrot Kodesh*, vol. 11 p. 109. For an overview of Rabbi Yosef Yitzchak's visit to the United States (and the Holy Land), see *Sefer Hasichot 5688-5691*, Introduction, p. 41.

here, *Oneness in Creation*, is the final discourse delivered in Chicago, and begins with the words *Kol Hamaarich B'echad*. It was delivered at a "gathering of Chasidim, *Anshei Chabad*, in the City of Chicago, at *Beit Hakneset Lubavitch, Motzaei Shabbat Kodesh Shemini*, 28 *Nissan* 5690 (1930)."[2]

Rabbi Yosef Yitzchak departed for Detroit the next morning, Sunday, *Erev Rosh Chodesh Iyar*. In a letter dated that day, from Detroit, he writes:

"...Shabbat-day I was introspective, thoughtful. I was to deliver a Chasidic discourse, say farewell, and share some words that would be remembered. Then I was to speak to a few people individually. This would be quite a task.

"At the close of Shabbat the Chasidim gathered at the Lubavitch *shul*. I arrived at nine o'clock, and delivered a Chasidic discourse entitled *Kol Hamaarich B'echad Maarichin Lo Yamav Ush'notav*. It took a half-hour or forty minutes, and the crowd was, thank G-d, large and attentive...

"Afterwards, I spoke for about fifteen minutes, sharing some heartfelt words. For seven minutes (I watched the clock—in every *shul* there is a large clock on the wall), I spoke of how small and low a human being can be... and how the teachings of Chasidus guide man in how to rid himself of all negative traits, and how to implant in their stead good traits, good deeds, compassion, and a pleasant disposition.

"In conclusion, I instructed that: 1) In every Chasidic *shul*, every day—weekday Shabbat and festival—*Tehillim* should be recited, as it is divided according to the days of the month. This should be followed by the recital of *Kaddish*. Other *shuls* are encouraged to adopt this custom as well. 2) Whoever considers himself part of the Chasidic community should study a portion of *Chumash* with *Rashi* every day."

Rabbi Yosef Yitzchak then describes how he addressed the en-

---

2. This is the text at the title of the discourse.

tire crowd, and in particular the young people, those already married and those preparing to start a family. He urged them to strengthen their commitment to Torah and *mitzvot* with the following words:

"…When one travels on a journey, he purchases a ticket which will take him to the station of his destination, and not further. We too have stations! 'Station *tefillin*,' 'station kosher,' 'station Shabbat,' 'station family sanctity.'

"To which station are *you* traveling? You don't don *tefillin*, you don't keep Shabbat, you don't eat kosher [food], you don't practice family sanctity! Until where do you expect to travel like this? You must know where you are and what will be the result of this. I appeal to you to form organizations, in which you will organize yourselves to uphold certain principles. I call upon you, and through you to all the youth of Chicago—establish yourself firmly and take the future of your family life in your hand, and you will be blissful."

[I concluded with] a heartfelt blessing to the crowd…: "Be well, and may we meet in good health with Moshiach in the Land of Israel!"

[One of the people responded:] "Have a safe journey and succeed! We are not parting from you. Your visit here will always remain fresh and warm with the good, warm fresh air that you brought to Chicago!"

It was a warm farewell—the entire *shul* and gallery were packed, and the atmosphere was filled with friendliness, a sweet and dignified love.

As I descended from the *bimah*, from all sides of the *shul* and gallery the crowd called out, "Have a safe, successful journey!"

The street was full; the police were in formation, as a huge crowd waited on the street. It was well-lit, and as I stood on the steps of the *shul* I could see the immense crowd. I said, "Be well and be successful in everything!"

I arrived back at my residence at 10:30.…

Thus ends Rabbi Yosef Yitzchak's account of his departure

from Chicago, the conclusion of a truly memorable and inspirational visit. His words have reverberated now for three-quarters of a century, touching countless lives, drawing untold Jews closer to their heritage—in Chicago, and around the world.

NOTE ON THE HEBREW TEXT: In vocalizing the Hebrew words in this edition we have followed the grammatical rules of the Holy Tongue, which occasionally differ from the traditional or colloquial pronunciation.

TRANSLATION
AND
COMMENTARY

Our Rabbis taught: *Hear, O Israel, the L-rd is our G-d, the L-rd is One.* Until here, concentration of the heart is required. These are the words of R. Meir. Rava said: The law accords with R. Meir.

Sumchos said: "Whoever prolongs [the pronunciation of the word] *Echad* (One) [in order to have proper intent] has his days and years prolonged."

Rav Acha bar Yaakov said: And that [letter of *Echad* requiring prolongation] is the *dalet*. Rav Ashi said: Provided that he does not hurry the [pronunciation of the letter] *chet*.

(Brachot 13b)

תָּנוּ רַבָּנָן: שְׁמַע יִשְׂרָאֵל ה׳ אֱלֹקֵינוּ ה׳ אֶחָד, עַד כָּאן צְרִיכָה כַּוָּונַת הַלֵּב, דִּבְרֵי רַבִּי מֵאִיר. אָמַר רָבָא, הֲלָכָה כְּרַבִּי מֵאִיר.

תַּנְיָא, סוּמְכוֹס אוֹמֵר: כָּל הַמַּאֲרִיךְ בְּאֶחָד מַאֲרִיכִין לוֹ יָמָיו וּשְׁנוֹתָיו.

אָמַר רַבִּי אַחָא בַּר יַעֲקֹב, וּבְדַלֵּית. אָמַר רַב אַשִׁי, וּבִלְבָד שֶׁלֹּא יַחְטוֹף בַּחֵית.

(ברכות יג:)

With the help of Heaven.
Gathering of Chasidim, *Anshei Chabad*, in the City of Chicago,
at *Beit Hakneset Lubavitch*.
Motzaei Shabbat Kodesh Shemini, 28 *Nissan*, 5690 (1930).

Whoever prolongs the [pronunciation of the word]
Echad (One)[1] has his days and years prolonged.
Rav Acha bar Yaakov said: And that [letter of *Echad*
requiring prolongation] is the [letter] *dalet*. Rav Ashi
said: Provided that he does not hurry the [pro-
nunciation of the letter] *chet* (*Brachot* 13b).

The underlying idea of stretching out the pronunciation of
the word *Echad* needs explanation, as does the reason why
one's years and days are prolonged as a result.

Now, the word *Echad* is comprised of three letters—*alef,
chet, dalet*, and we are to protract the enunciation of the *dalet*,
providing we do not hasten our pronunciation of the *chet*. We
need to clarify the idea of stretching out the *dalet*, and Rav
Ashi's caveat not to slur the letter *chet*, from which it is understood that the protraction of the *dalet* must not be at the ex-
pense of shortening the *chet*.

THE BERAITA

The teaching of *Whoever prolongs the Echad...* comes in con-
tinuation to the following *Beraita*:[2]
Hear, O Israel, Havaya[3] *is our G-d, Havaya is One.*[4] Until
here [i.e., until the end of the first verse of *Shema*], concentration of the heart is required. These are the words of R. Meir.
Rava said: The law accords with R. Meir.[5]

---

1. This refers to the last word of the
verse *Shema Yisrael Hashem Elokeinu
Hashem Echad* (Hear O Israel, the
L-rd is our G-d, the L-rd is One), recited twice daily in our prayers. The
idea of prolonging the word *Echad* is
to assist in one's concentration.

2. BERAITA. Collection of laws and ex-
positions compiled or originated by
the Sages following the completion of
the *Mishnah*. These Sages include R.
Chiya, R. Oshiya, R. Elazar ben Yaakov, R. Yishmael and R. Akiva.
    The word *Beraita* is derived from

בס״ד. אסיפת אגודת חסידים אנשי חב״ד
בעי״ת טשיקאגא בבהכנ״ס ליובאוויטש.
מוצש״ק שמיני כ״ח ניסן. תר צדיק.

כָּל הַמַּאֲרִיךְ בְּאֶחָד מַאֲרִיכִין לוֹ יָמָיו וּשְׁנוֹתָיו. אָמַר רַבִּי
אַחָא בַּר יַעֲקֹב וּבְדִ׳ דְּהָאֲרִיכוּת בְּאֶחָד צְרִיכָה לִהְיוֹת
בְּהַדַּלֵּית, אָמַר רַב אַשִׁי וּבִלְבָד שֶׁלֹּא יַחְטוֹף בַּחֵית, (ברכות
י״ג ב׳).

וְצָרִיךְ לְהָבִין מַהוּ עִנְיַן הָאֲרִיכוּת בְּאֶחָד, וּמַהוּ אֲרִיכוּת
יָמִים וְשָׁנִים דְּמִי שֶׁהוּא מַאֲרִיךְ בְּאֶחָד מַאֲרִיכִין לוֹ יָמָיו
וּשְׁנוֹתָיו.

דְּהִנֵּה תֵּיבַת אֶחָד הוּא בַּת ג׳ אוֹתִיּוֹת, א׳ח׳ד׳, וְהָאֲרִיכוּת
הוּא בְּהַדִ׳ וּבִלְבָד שֶׁלֹּא יַחְטוֹף גַּם אֶת הַחִ׳, וְצָרִיךְ לְהָבִין מַהוּ
הָאֲרִיכוּת בְּהַדִ׳ וְאַזְהָרָתוֹ שֶׁל רַב אַשִׁי שֶׁלֹּא יַחְטוֹף אֶת הַחֵית.
דְּמִכָּל זֶה מוּבָן דְּהָאֲרִיכוּת בְּהַדִ׳ הוּא דַּוְקָא כְּשֶׁאֵינוֹ חוֹטֵף אֶת
הַחִ׳.

וְהִנֵּה מַאֲמָר זֶה דְּכָל הַמַּאֲרִיךְ בְּאֶחָד הוּא הֶמְשֵׁךְ
הַבְּרַיְיתָא

דְּתָנוּ רַבָּנָן שְׁמַע יִשְׂרָאֵל הוי׳ אֱלֹקֵינוּ הוי׳ אֶחָד עַד כָּאן
צְרִיכִים כַּוְּונַת הַלֵּב דִּבְרֵי רַבִּי מֵאִיר, אָמַר רָבָא וַהֲלָכָה כְּרַבִּי
מֵאִיר.

---

the Aramaic word *bara*, meaning "outside," implying that they were taught by the *Tannaim* outside of the study hall of R. Yehuda Hanassi—the redactor of the *Mishnah*.

3. The colloquial form of The In-

effable Divine Name, or Tetragrammaton, composed of the four letters Y-H-V-H.

4. Deuteronomy 6:4.

5. *Brachot*, ibid.

To summarize: The *Beraita* teach-

TWO CONCENTRATIONS

There are two types of concentration: concentration of the mind and concentration of the heart. Mental concentration entails intellectual comprehension—exerting one's mind to understand and grasp a concept until one has it firmly pinned down and understands it in all of its details. Concentration of the heart means bringing one's clear understanding of the concept from its abstract plane to an applied one, with the cultivation of fine character traits.[6]

Initially, a person should direct his efforts to unearth any personality trait that is not good—and certainly any that is loathsome—and then to uproot the trait thoroughly. Anything improper, whether in his relationship with people or with G-d, should be repulsed by him. All of his energy and efforts should be focused on implanting in himself commendable traits and proper behavior. This, then, is the meaning of "concentration of the heart": steering his heart, since "the heart distributes to all the limbs,"[7] to bring every fine quality into actuality.

HAVAYA AND ELOKIM

Now the recital of *Hear O Israel...One* is a call for our awareness and comprehension of the Creator's Oneness. The words *Hear O Israel* mean that the Jew should perceive, understand and apprehend (*hear*) that *Havaya* is *Elokeinu* (our G-d): that *Elokeinu*, i.e., our power and our life, is *Havaya*.[8] The Divine

---

es us that the first verse of *Shema* must be said with "concentration of the heart"; the Talmud adds that the word *Echad* of this verse should be protracted; Rav Acha bar Yaakov clarifies that this refers specifically to the letter *dalet* of the word *Echad*; and Rav Ashi cautions against hurrying the pronunciation of the letter *chet*. All of these statements will be expounded upon in this discourse.

6. I.e., one takes his knowledge and translates it into practice, into re-

fining his character.

7. See *Likkutei Torah, Shir Hashirim* 29b from *Zohar* III:161b: "The heart is the seat of one's blood—the soul and energy of one's body. The food one eats becomes digested and turns into blood. The liver takes most of it and transmits the choicest part to the heart, which in turn, distributes it to all the limbs." In our context, this phrase is used to indicate that the concentration of the heart is to subsequently be applied to the whole

וְהִנֵּה יֶשְׁנוֹ כַּוָּנַת הַמּוֹחַ וְכַוָּנַת הַלֵּב, כַּוָּנַת הַמּוֹחַ הִיא
הַשָּׂגָה שִׂכְלִית מַה שֶׁמַּגִּיעַ מוֹחוֹ לְהָבִין וּלְהַשִּׂיג עִנְיָן שִׂכְלִי
עַד שֶׁיַּעֲמוֹד עָלָיו וִיבִינוֹ בְּכָל פְּרָטֵי עִנְיָנָיו, וְכַוָּנַת הַלֵּב
הוּא לְהָבִיא הַשָּׂגָתוֹ הַטּוֹבָה מֵהַכֹּחַ אֶל הַפּוֹעַל בְּמִדּוֹת
טוֹבוֹת,

וְהַיְינוּ דְּרֵאשִׁית עֲבוֹדָתוֹ תִּהְיֶה לַחְקוֹר אַחַר כָּל מִדָּה לֹא
טוֹבָה וּמִכָּל שֶׁכֵּן מִדָּה מְגוּנָה לְעָקְרָהּ וּלְשָׁרְשָׁהּ אֲשֶׁר בַּל
תֵּרָאֶה וּבַל תִּמָּצֵא, וְהַדָּבָר הֲלֹא טוֹב בֵּין אִם הוּא דָבָר שֶׁבֵּין
אָדָם לַמָּקוֹם וּבֵין אִם הוּא דָבָר אֲשֶׁר בֵּין אָדָם לַחֲבֵירוֹ, יִהְיֶה
מָאוּס אֶצְלוֹ, וְכָל יְגִיעָתוֹ וְהִשְׁתַּדְּלוּתוֹ יִהְיֶה לִנְטוֹעַ בְּעַצְמוֹ
מִדּוֹת טוֹבוֹת וְהַנְהָגוֹת יְשָׁרוֹת וְזֶהוּ כַּוָּנַת הַלֵּב לְכַוֵּין אֶת
לִבּוֹ, דְּלִיבָּא פָּלִיג לְכָל לְכָל שַׁיְּיפִין לְהָבִיא כָּל מִדָּה טוֹבָה לְפוֹעַל
מַמָּשׁ.

וְהִנֵּה אֲמִירַת שְׁמַע יִשְׂרָאֵל כוּ' אֶחָד הוּא יְדִיעַת וְהַשָּׂגַת
אַחְדוּת הַבּוֹרֵא בָּרוּךְ הוּא דְּזֶהוּ פֵּירוּשׁ שְׁמַע יִשְׂרָאֵל,
שֶׁהַיִּשְׂרָאֵל יִשְׁמַע וְיָבִין וְיַשִּׂיג כִּי הוי' אֱלֹקֵינוּ, דֶּאֱלֹקֵינוּ הַיְינוּ
כֹּחֵינוּ וְחַיּוּתֵנוּ הוּא הוי'. דְּהִנֵּה שֵׁם אֱלֹקִים הוּא לְשׁוֹן כֹּחַ

---

body in actual deed—perfecting all parts of one's character.

To explain this further: When one meditates on a G-dly matter and is intellectually inspired, this inspiration has not yet affected his entire body. However, when this inspiration flows from head to heart, then one's entire body is inspired, for the heart is at the center of the body—it distributes to all limbs and awakens the entire body. (*Torah Or* 8a; *Maamarei Admur Hatzemach Tzedek—Hanachot 5615*, p. 233; *B'Shaah Shehikdimu 5672* vol. 2, p. 1015 ff.; *Likkutei Sichot* vol. 37, p. 160 and vol. 39, p. 42. See also discourse entitled *L'havin Inyan Pesach U'matzah, 5728*, ch. 2 and sources cited there.)

8. HAVAYA, ELOKIM: There are many Hebrew names for G-d in Scripture, each of which expresses a different aspect or attribute of the Divinity. *Havaya* refers to G-d the Infinite, transcending creation and nature, time and space completely—the aspect of Divinity that brings everything into existence *ex nihilo*; the life-force of all of creation.

Elokim, conversely, represents the aspect of G-d which *conceals* the In-name of *Elokim* denotes power, as seen from the verse, "He has also taken away the mighty [*eilei*] of the land,"[9] denoting power and strength. In addition, the word *Elokim* and the word *hateva* (the nature) are numerically equivalent,[10] for the nature of something is also its power.[11]

We declare *Havaya Elokeinu*: the power and life-force of the Jewish people is *Havaya*, a force that transcends nature. Nature is limited by time and by space. That which is delineated by space is delimited by its boundaries.[12] Likewise, something delineated by time is restricted by the boundaries of past, present and future. *Havaya*, however, indicates that He was, is and will be—simultaneously, for He transcends space and transcends time.[13]

This is the import of the words *Havaya Elokeinu*—the nature of the Jewish people is to elicit into the limitations of time-and-space the [G-dly] light[14] and revelation that transcends time-and-space.[15]

*   *   *

---

finite Light and life-force, since this Infinite force is too intense for finite creatures to endure. *Elokim* is the power of G-d that makes the world appear as though it exists naturally and independently by itself. (*Elokim* therefore has the numerical value of the word *hateva*, nature.)

This, the discourse will soon explain, is the meaning of the verse *Havaya Elokeinu*: *Havaya* **is** *Elokim*. Though every creature feels its own independence (*Elokim*), in reality it is animated entirely by G-d's life-force (*Havaya*). Thus, "nature" is indeed *supernatural*.

[It's interesting to note that this theme appears in other discourses delivered around this time—in *Ma'ayan Ganim*, on 10 Shevat, and *Mayim Rabbim*, on 24 Shevat. (See also *Sefer Hamaamarim Melukat*, vol. 4, p. 49, and footnote 56 there.)]

9. Ezekiel 17:13. The words *Elokim* and *eilei* ("mighty") share the same root—"*eil*" (אֵל).

10. Each letter of the Hebrew alphabet has a numeric value. The first nine letters, from *alef* through *tet*, equal one through nine respectively. The next nine letters, *yud* through *tzaddik*, equal ten through ninety respectively. The next four letters, *kuf* through *tav*, equal one hundred through four hundred respectively.

(Other numbers are created by combining single Hebrew characters of different value. For example, one hundred and twenty-three would be *kuf chaf gimmel* — קכג. Five-hundred is represented by *tav kuf* — תק , six-hundred by *tav reish* — תר, nine-hundred by *tav tav kuf* — תתק, etc. One thousand is represented by a single letter followed by an apostrophe.

וּכְמוֹ שֶׁכָּתוּב וְאֶת אֵילֵי הָאָרֶץ לָקָח שְׁמוֹרֶה עַל הַכֹּחַ וְהַחוֹזֶק, וֶאֱלֹקִים בְּגִימַטְרִיָּא הַטֶּבַע שֶׁבְּכָל דָּבָר וְדָבָר הֲרֵי טִבְעוֹ הוּא כֹּחוֹ.

וְאָנוּ אוֹמְרִים הוי׳ אֱלֹקֵינוּ, דְּהַכֹּחַ וְהַחַיּוּת דְּיִשְׂרָאֵל הוּא הוי׳, הַיְינוּ מַה שֶּׁלְּמַעְלָה מֵהַטֶּבַע דְּטֶבַע הוּא הַמּוּגְדָּר בִּזְמַן וּמָקוֹם, דְּהַמּוּגְדָּר בְּמָקוֹם הוּא מוּגְבָּל בְּהַגְבָּלוֹתָיו, וְכֵן הוּא בִּזְמַן שֶׁמּוּגְבָּל בְּהַגְבָּלָה דְּעָבַר הֹוֶה וְעָתִיד, וַהוי׳ הוּא הָיָה הֹוֶה וְיִהְיֶה כְּאֶחָד שֶׁהוּא לְמַעְלָה מִן הַמָּקוֹם וּלְמַעְלָה מִן הַזְּמַן.

וְזֶהוּ הוי׳ אֱלֹקֵינוּ דְּהַטֶּבַע דְּיִשְׂרָאֵל הוּא דְּבִהַהַגְבָּלוֹת דִּזְמַן וּמָקוֹם יַמְשִׁיכוּ הָאוֹר וְהַגִּילוּי שֶׁלְּמַעְלָה מִזְמַן וּמָקוֹם.

* * *

For example, 1001 would be written: *alef' alef* — אא.)

The Hebrew letters that spell *El-okim* are of equal numerical value to the letters that spell *hateva*.

11. Everything that exists is enlivened by a specific G-dly life-force uniquely its own. This life-force is the "spiritual DNA" of that given entity—that which defines the parameters and nature of its existence. Therefore, the nature of any given entity directly reflects the spiritual power or life-force that enlivens it. That is why the Hebrew words for nature (*hateva*) and Divine power (*Elokim*) are numerically equivalent, since they are one and the same—*the nature of something is also its power* (life-force).

12. I.e., it is bound by its spatial limitations.

13. *Havaya* represents the aspect of G-dliness that transcends the limits of time and space. Indeed, the word *Havaya* implies *haya, hoveh, v'yihyeh* ("G-d *is, was*, and *will be*")—a G-dly realm where past, present and future exist simultaneously (*Zohar* III:257b in *Raya Mehemna*).

14. LIGHT. Obviously, this does not refer to physical light. In the language of the mystics, light refers to the effusion of Divine "energy." (The mystics prefer light as the metaphor for G-d's "energy" for a number of reasons. Among them: light must remain attached to its source in order to exist; light is not affected by its surroundings; the effusion of light causes no depletion in the luminary. See Schochet, *Mystical Concepts in Chassidism* (Kehot, 1988).)

15. Through one's spiritual service

ECHAD VS. YACHID

The understanding and comprehension that *Havaya* is *El-okeinu*—that our power and life-force is *Havaya* Who transcends time-and-space—is attained by contemplating the Oneness of G-d.

The meaning of *Echad* is *One*, similar to the definition of the word *Yachid*, which means *Singular*. The difference, though, between *Echad* and *Yachid* is that *Yachid* connotes Singular in essence, while *Echad* connotes Oneness that is discerned from the particulars of the created beings and the vivification [of creation].[16] In other words, by contemplating G-d's Oneness, we attain this recognition of *Havaya El-okeinu*—that our power and life force is *Havaya*.[17]

Thus, the recital of *Shema Yisrael* entails concentration of the mind. So why does R. Meir say, "Until here concentration of the *heart* is required"?

DARK THEN LIGHT

To understand the solution to the above, we need to first present an elucidation of the word *Echad*.

The verse says, "And it was evening and it was morning, one day (*yom echad*)."[18] This "*one* day" incorporates, specifically, both an evening and a morning. For the 24 hours of a day include 12 hours of nighttime and 12 hours of daytime, which make the day complete, since by definition, a day has an evening and a morning, and the evening precedes the morning.[19]

---

one demonstrates that creation is not just defined by its restrictions of time and space, but rather by the truth it reflects—the truth of the Infinite G-d, who wished to create a world upon which man would fulfill his will by learning His Torah and keeping His *mitzvot*. See p. 32 ff.

16. See p. 36 and references in footnote 49.

To explain the difference between the word *yachid* ("singular") and the word *echad* ("one"):

"Singular" means that there is *only one*. "One," however, can also mean *the first of many*. For example, when counting several items we say "one, two, three…", using the term "one" to indicate the *first* item. It would therefore seem more appropriate to use the term *Yachid* ("Singular") when speaking of (*the One and Only*) G-d; why, then, does Scripture state *Havaya Ech-*

וְהִנֵּה יְדִיעַת וְהַשָּׂגַת דָּבָר זֶה שֶׁהוי׳ אֱלֹקֵינוּ, דְּכֹחֵנוּ וְחַיּוּתֵנוּ הוּא הוי׳ שֶׁלְּמַעְלָה מִזְּמַן וּמָקוֹם הוּא בָּא עַל יְדֵי הַהִתְבּוֹנְנוּת בַּהוי׳ אֶחָד.

כִּי אֶחָד פֵּירוּשׁוֹ הוּא אײנֶער כְּמוֹ יָחִיד דְּפֵירוּשׁוֹ אײנצִיג, אֶלָּא דְּהַהֶפְרֵשׁ בֵּין אֶחָד לְיָחִיד הוּא, דְּיָחִיד הוּא שֶׁמְּיוּחָד בְּעַצֶם, וְאֶחָד הוּא שֶׁהָאַחְדוּת נִיכֶּרֶת מִפְּרָטֵי הַנִּבְרָאִים וְהַהִתְהַוּוּת, וְהַיְינוּ דְּעַל יְדֵי הַהִתְבּוֹנְנוּת בַּהוי׳ אֶחָד הִנֵּה עַל יְדֵי זֶה בָּאִים לִידֵי הַכָּרָה זוֹ דַּהוי׳ אֱלֹקֵינוּ, דְּכֹחֵינוּ וְחַיּוּתֵנוּ הוּא הוי׳.

וְאִם כֵּן הֲרֵי אֲמִירַת שְׁמַע יִשְׂרָאֵל הוּא כַּוָּונַת הַמּוֹחַ, וְלָמָּה אָמַר רַבִּי מֵאִיר דְּעַד כַּאן צְרִיכִים כַּוָּונַת הַלֵּב,

וּלְהָבִין זֶה צָרִיךְ לְהַקְדִּים תְּחִלָּה פֵּירוּשׁ אֶחָד,

הִנֵּה כְּתִיב וַיְהִי עֶרֶב וַיְהִי בֹקֶר יוֹם אֶחָד, דְּיוֹם אֶחָד הוּא כְּשֶׁכָּלוּל מֵעֶרֶב וּבֹקֶר דַּוְקָא, דְּכ״ד שָׁעוֹת הַיּוֹם הֵן י״ב שָׁעוֹת הַלַּיְלָה וְי״ב שָׁעוֹת הַיּוֹם וְאָז הוּא יוֹם שָׁלֵם, דְּהֶגְדֵּר הַיּוֹם הוּא שֶׁהוּא מוּגְדָּר בְּהַהַגְדָּרָה דְּעֶרֶב וּבֹקֶר וְשֶׁהָעֶרֶב יִהְיֶה קָדוּם לַבֹּקֶר,

---

ad ("G-d is *One*"), a term that indicates the potential for plurality?

Chasidus explains that this in fact is the verse's emphasis: That even within the *plurality* of creation, "G-d is *One*"—absolute Oneness. (This idea would have been lost had the verse said, *Havaya Yachid* ("G-d is Singular"); that would have been understood to be referring to G-d as He completely transcends creation. The point of this verse, however, is to speak of G-d's Oneness even as He is within creation.) See *Torah Or*, 55b; *Derech Mitzvotecha* 124a.

17. The verse is thus interpreted as follows: *Shema Yisrael*—Understand, Israel, that *Havaya Elokeinu*—our very nature is supernatural. Why? Because *Havaya Echad*—G-d's transcendent Oneness pervades the plurality of creation.

Obviously, then, this verse contains a deep and powerful message and requires intense concentration.

18. Genesis 1:5.

19. As is apparent from the aforementioned verse, "It was evening…and morning, one day."

In other words, in order for there to be morning light,[20] there must be an evening that precedes it. And by dint of one's labor in the evening, one reaches the light of morning.[21]

The reason for this [order] is that G-d first thought to create the world through the Attribute of Judgment, but He foresaw that the world would not be able to endure, so He merged it [the Attribute of Judgment] with the Attribute of Mercy,[22] as the saying, "At the beginning, darkness; then light."[23] So it was at the creation of the world. At first, it is written, "In the beginning *Elokim* created the heavens and the earth,"[24] since the creation and vivification of the worlds, in actuality, is through the Divine name of *Elokim*, which is identified with the Attribute of Judgment and with the *tzimtzum*[25] [of G-d's light]—"At the beginning, darkness." Later it is written, "On the day that *Havaya Elokim* made earth and heaven"[26]—"then light." The state of "then light" can be attained only through the preceding state of "at the beginning, darkness."[27]

HAVAYA AND ELOKIM = SUN AND SHIELD

[To explain:] It is written, "For *Havaya Elokim* is a sun and a shield."[28] The two names of *Havaya Elokim*, which refer to G-d as He is imminent in nature and as He transcends nature, respectively, are analogous to the sun and to the sun's

---

20. Cf. Genesis 44:3.

21. In Kabbalistic and Chasidic terminology, "evening" refers to a condition of spiritual darkness, when G-dliness is not apparent. "Morning," the time of light, indicates a condition of Divine manifestation—G-dly light. Thus, the fact that evening precedes morning (in the unit of "day") is quite significant: it indicates that one can only reach spiritual light through first battling the darkness. True G-dly revelation is only born of one's struggle with the forces that at-

tempt to conceal G-dliness.

22. See *Rashi*, Genesis 1:1; *Midrash Rabbah* 12:15; ibid., 14:1.

The Attributes of Judgment and Mercy are not to be understood solely in their literal sense, in the context of reward and punishment—that G-d initially thought to be strict with creation, and then decided to be more lenient—but rather in a more metaphorical sense, referring to different states of G-dliness, as the discourse will explain. Judgment refers to the "restricting" of G-dliness, a state of

וְהַיְינוּ דִּבְכְדֵי שֶׁיִּהְיֶה בֹּקֶר אוֹר צָרִיךְ לִהְיוֹת תְּחִלָּה עֶרֶב
וְעַל יְדֵי הָעֲבוֹדָה בְּהָעֶרֶב עַל יְדֵי זֶה מַגִּיעִים לְהַבֹּקֶר אוֹר.

וְטַעַם הַדָּבָר הוּא דִּבַתְחִלָּה עָלָה בְּמַחֲשָׁבָה לִבְרוֹא אֶת
הָעוֹלָם בְּמִדַּת הַדִּין רָאָה שֶׁאֵין הָעוֹלָם יָכוֹל לְהִתְקַיֵּם שִׁיתֵּף
עִמּוֹ מִדַּת הָרַחֲמִים, וּכְמַאֲמָר בְּרֵישָׁא חֲשׁוֹכָא וַהֲדַר נְהוֹרָא, וְכֵן
הָיָה בִּבְרִיאַת הָעוֹלָם דְּתְחִלָּה כְּתִיב בְּרֵאשִׁית בָּרָא אֱלֹקִים אֶת
הַשָּׁמַיִם וְאֵת הָאָרֶץ דִּבְרִיאַת וְהִתְהַוּוּת הָעוֹלָמוֹת בְּהִתְהַוּוּת
בְּפוֹעַל הוּא עַל יְדֵי שֵׁם אֱלֹקִים שֶׁהוּא מִדַּת הַדִּין וְהַצִּמְצוּם
דְּבְרֵישָׁא חֲשׁוֹכָא וְאַחַר כַּךְ כְּתִיב בְּיוֹם עֲשׂוֹת הוי׳ אֱלֹקִים אֶרֶץ
וְשָׁמַיִם שֶׁהוּא וַהֲדַר נְהוֹרָא. וּבְכְדֵי שֶׁיִּהְיֶה אַחַר כַּךְ וַהֲדַר
נְהוֹרָא הוּא עַל יְדֵי בְּרֵישָׁא חֲשׁוֹכָא,

דְּהִנֵּה כְּתִיב כִּי שֶׁמֶשׁ וּמָגֵן הוי׳ אֱלֹקִים דְּהַב׳ שֵׁמוֹת הוי׳
אֱלֹקִים שֶׁהוּא הַטֶּבַע וּלְמַעֲלָה מֵהַטֶּבַע הוּא כְּדוּגְמַת הַשֶּׁמֶשׁ
וּמָגֵן הַשֶּׁמֶשׁ, דְּהִנֵּה זֶה מַה שֶׁאָנוּ רוֹאִים אֶת הַשֶּׁמֶשׁ הֲלֹא אָנוּ

Divine concealment (darkness, *tzimtzum*), while Mercy refers to G-dly manifestation, a state of Divine revelation (light). Generally speaking, these two states (Divine concealment and revelation) are synonymous with *Elokim* and *Havaya*, respectively.

For a more comprehensive analysis of this topic see *Yom Tov Shel Rosh Hashanah 5659, Discourse One*, p. 23 ff. (Kehot, 2000).

23. *Shabbat* 77b. The Talmud states regarding Creation that "first [it was] dark; then [it was] light," in accordance with Genesis 1:2-3.

24. Genesis 1:1.

25. TZIMTZUM. Self-contraction or self-limitation of the infinite revelation of G-d—the *Or Ein Sof*—which allows finite worlds to exist. Prior to creation, there was only the Infinite light filling all existence. Within this infinite revelation, finite worlds and beings could not possibly exist. When it arose in G-d's will to create the worlds and all their inhabitants, He contracted and concealed the Infinite light, creating a "void" in which finite existence can endure. This concealment of G-d's Infinite light is analogous to darkness.

26. Genesis 2:4.

27. This concept will be explained further.

28. Psalms 84:12.

shield.[29] For when we look at the sun, we don't actually see the sun itself. We see only its shield, its sheath, which covers the orb of the sun. The earth and its denizens can tolerate the sun's light and radiance only because of its cloaking shield and sheath. This [shield] enables the light to be received and to effect the results that it does—as it is written, "With the sweetness of the produce of the sun, and with the sweetness of the moon's yield."[30] Accordingly, the resultant effects come about through the sun itself as it is concealed and hidden in its shield and covering, so that its light can be tolerated and produce its intended effects.[31]

* * *

HAVAYA AND ELOKIM IN CREATION

The [above scriptural] metaphor helps us understand how this concept applies in the spiritual realm to the two Divine names of *Elokim* and *Havaya*. In truth, the creation [of the world] originates from the name *Havaya*. It is the name *Havaya* that creates. As it is written, "[They shall praise the name of *Havaya*,] for He has commanded, and they were created"[32]—the entire creation of the worlds and the creatures comes from the name of *Havaya*.

Nevertheless, if the name of *Havaya* were the instrument through which the creation took place *in actuality*, then it would not have created our present physical form of existence.[33] Instead, the existence of all beings would have been utterly abnegated, like the nullification of the sun's rays within the sun. And Divinity would not have been sensed by created beings, or recognized and grasped as it is now.[34]

THE PURPOSE OF CREATION

It is written, "Who in His goodness, renews each day, con-

---

29. That the sun has a "sheath" independent of itself can be seen from *Nedarim* 9b: "In the World to Come, G-d will remove the sun from its sheath."

speaks of the sweetness added to the produce by sunlight—a benefit that is possible only because of the shield that tempers the sun's naturally overpowering strength. See *Rashi* there.

30. Deuteronomy 33:14. This verse

31. I.e., the sun's *concealment* allows

רוֹאִים רַק אֶת הַמָּגֵן וְנַרְתֵּק שֶׁמְכַסֶּה עַל מְאוֹר הַשֶּׁמֶשׁ, דְּמָאוֹר
הַשֶּׁמֶשׁ עַצְמוֹ לֹא הָיָה בְּאֶפְשָׁרוּת הָעוֹלָם וְהַנִּבְרָאִים לְקַבֵּל
אוֹרוֹ וְזִיווֹ וְרַק עַל יְדֵי כִּסּוּי הַמָּגֵן וְנַרְתֵּק עַל יְדֵי זֶה יוּכַל
לְהִתְקַבֵּל וּפוֹעֵל פְּעוּלָתוֹ כְּמוֹ שֶׁכָּתוּב מִמֶּגֶד תְּבוּאוֹת שָׁמֶשׁ
וּמִמֶּגֶד גֶּרֶשׁ יְרָחִים אִם כֵּן הֲרֵי הַפְּעוּלָה בָּאָה מֵעֶצֶם הַשֶּׁמֶשׁ
שֶׁמִּתְעַלֵּם וּמִסְתַּתֵּר בְּהַמָּגֵן וְנַרְתֵּק בִּכְדֵי שֶׁיּוּכַל לְהִתְקַבֵּל
וְלִפְעוֹל פְּעוּלָתוֹ.

* * *

וְהַדּוּגְמָא מִזֶּה יוּבַן לְמַעְלָה בְּב׳ הַשֵּׁמוֹת דְּשֵׁם אֱלֹקִים וְשֵׁם
הוי׳ דְּבֶאֱמֶת הַהִתְהַוּוּת הוּא מִשֵּׁם הוי׳ דְּשֵׁם הוי׳ הוּא הַמְהַוֶּוה
כְּמוֹ שֶׁכָּתוּב כִּי הוּא צִוָּה וְנִבְרָאוּ דְּכָל הַהִתְהַוּוּת דְּעוֹלָמוֹת
וְנִבְרָאִים הוּא מִשֵּׁם הוי׳,

אַךְ אִם הָיָה הַהִתְהַוּוּת בְּפוֹעַל עַל יְדֵי שֵׁם הוי׳ אָז לֹא
הָיְתָה הַהִתְהַוּוּת בִּמְצִיאוּת יֵשׁ גַּשְׁמִי כְּמוֹ שֶׁהוּא עַתָּה אֶלָּא
הָיָה כָּל מְצִיאוּתָן בְּטֵלִים בְּתַכְלִית הַבִּיטוּל כְּבִיטוּל זִיו
הַשֶּׁמֶשׁ בְּהַשֶּׁמֶשׁ וְלֹא הָיָה הָאֱלֹקוּת יִתְבָּרֵךְ נִרְגָּשׁ בַּנִּבְרָאִים
וְנִיכָּר וּמוּשָׂג בְּהַכָּרָתָן וְהַשָּׂגָתָן כְּמוֹ שֶׁהוּא עַתָּה,

וּכְתִיב הַמְחַדֵּשׁ בְּטוּבוֹ בְּכָל יוֹם תָּמִיד מַעֲשֵׂה בְרֵאשִׁית,

---

it to produce its intended effect: that its light be beneficial to earth.

32. Psalms 148:5.

33. *Havaya* is the Divine name connoting (intense) G-dly revelation. Were creation to stem solely from *Havaya*, there would be no possibility for the creation of independent, physical beings—beings that do not naturally recognize their G-dly source—since G-dliness would pervade all of "existence." Instead, all of creation would be completely subsumed in G-d's Infinite light. It is only through the concealment of G-dliness—*Elokim*—that independent creatures can emerge. (And these creatures ultimately fulfill the Divine purpose in creation, as will be explained.)

34. Since there would be no independent beings to do so.

tinuously the work of creation."[35] The work of creation is re-
newed because of His attribute of goodness and kindness, as
"the nature of the benevolent is to do good."[36] For "the Holy
One, blessed be He, desired a dwelling place in the lower
realms,"[37] to create and to bring into existence a physical universe that would appear to be an independent entity and being; and in this world, to create man with a physical body,
into which He would lower a divine soul, endowing it with
the force and strength to overcome the body's corporeality and
vanquish all of the body's fleshly desires, through the power of
Torah [study] and the "service of the heart" of prayer.[38]

   The Torah was given to us in this lowly terrestrial physical plane. Although the angels had wanted the Torah for
themselves, as it is written, "You Who has set Your majesty
upon the heavens,"[39] Moses countered, "Do you [angels] have
an evil inclination!?"[40] So the Torah was given specifically to
man, who possesses a physical body, with an evil inclination
that entices him—with numerous manners of deceit—trying
to lure him off the proper path. But by studying Torah and
observing it, the Torah's inner-luminous core enlightens him
in the paths of [true] life, eternal life—as the saying, "Eternal
life You planted within us."[41] That is, through the practical

---

35. Liturgy, morning blessings of the
Shema.

36. See R. Tzvi Hirsch Ashkenazi,
Chacham Tzvi (Responsa), Sec. 18;
R. Yosef Irgas, *Shomer Emumim*,
2:14, quoting the Kabbalists. See also
Likkutei Sichot vol. 24, p. 334 in foot-
note.

37. *Tanchuma, Nasso* 16.

38. See *Taanit* 2a: "'To serve Him
with all your heart' (Deuteronomy
11:13). What is 'service of the heart'?
This is prayer."

39. Psalms 8:2.

40. See *Shabbat* 88b: When Moshe
ascended on High, the ministering
angels asked G-d, "Why is there a human amongst us?" "He came to receive the Torah," replied G-d. "The
hidden treasure that was hidden from
before Creation [i.e., the To-
rah]—you wish to give to humans?!"
exclaimed the angels. "What is man
that You should remember him, son
of man that You should be mindful
of him? L-rd our Master, how mighty
is Your Name throughout the earth,
You Who has set Your majesty upon
the heavens!" (Psalms 8:5, 2). [You

דְזֶה מַה שֶׁמַּעֲשֵׂה בְרֵאשִׁית הֵם בְּהִתְחַדְּשׁוּת הוּא מִצַּד מִדַּת
טוּבוֹ וְחַסְדּוֹ יִתְבָּרֵךְ דְּטֶבַע הַטּוֹב לְהֵיטִיב כִּי נִתְאַוָּה
הַקָּדוֹשׁ בָּרוּךְ הוּא לִהְיוֹת לוֹ יִתְבָּרֵךְ דִּירָה בַּתַּחְתּוֹנִים
לִבְרוֹא וּלְהַוּוֹת עוֹלָם גַּשְׁמִי שֶׁיִּהְיֶה נִרְאֶה לְיֵשׁ וּמְצִיאוּת
וּבְעוֹלָם זֶה לִבְרוֹא אֶת הָאָדָם בַּעַל גּוּף גַּשְׁמִי וּלְהוֹרִיד
נְשָׁמָה אֱלֹקִית וְלִיתֵּן לָהּ כֹּחַ וָעוֹז לְהִתְגַּבֵּר עַל חוּמְרִיּוּת
הַגּוּף וְלִכְבּוֹשׁ אֶת כָּל תַּאֲוֹתָיו עַל יְדֵי כֹּחַ הַתּוֹרָה וְהָעֲבוֹדָה
שֶׁבַּלֵּב בִּתְפִלָּה,

דְהַתּוֹרָה נִיתְּנָה לְמַטָּה בָּאָרֶץ הַלֵּזוּ הַגַּשְׁמִית, דְּכַאֲשֶׁר
הַמַּלְאָכִים בִּקְּשׁוּ אֶת הַתּוֹרָה כְּמוֹ שֶׁכָּתוּב אֲשֶׁר תְּנָה הוֹדְךָ
עַל הַשָּׁמָיִם הֵשִׁיב לָהֶם מֹשֶׁה כְּלוּם יֵצֶר הָרָע יֵשׁ בָּכֶם
וְנִיתְּנָה דַּוְקָא לְבַעֲלֵי גוּף גַּשְׁמִי שֶׁיֵּשׁ בָּהֶם יֵצֶר הָרָע דְּהַיֵּצֶר
הָרָע מֵסִית וּמַדִּיחַ אֶת הָאָדָם בְּכַמָּה מִינֵי עַרְמוּמִיּוֹת לַהֲסִיתוֹ
וּלְהַדִּיחוֹ מִדֶּרֶךְ הַיָּשָׁר, הִנֵּה עַל יְדֵי לִימוּד הַתּוֹרָה וְקִיּוּמָהּ
הִנֵּה הַמָּאוֹר שֶׁבָּהּ מְאִירָה לּוֹ לְהָאָדָם בְּדַרְכֵי הַחַיִּים בְּחַיֵּי
עוֹלָם כְּמַאֲמָר וְחַיֵּי עוֹלָם נָטַע בְּתוֹכֵנוּ, וְהַיְינוּ דְּעַל יְדֵי זֶה
שֶׁהָאָדָם עוֹשֶׂה בְּפוֹעַל בְּקִיּוּם הַמִּצְוֹת מַעֲשִׂיּוֹת הֲרֵי הוּא

---

set your might upon the earth to punish the wickedness of man; how, then, can you give man Your precious Torah? "Set Your majesty [Torah] upon the heavens!"—*Maharsha*.]

Said G-d to Moshe: "Answer them!" Moshe replied, "But I am afraid lest they burn me with their breath." G-d replied, "Hold on to My throne and answer them!" ... Moshe said, "Master of the Universe, the Torah you are about to give us—what is written in it? 'I am the L-rd your G-d who took you out of Egypt.'" Turning to the angels he asked, "Did *you* descend to Egypt? Were *you* enslaved? Then why should you receive the Torah? What else is written in it? ... 'Do not kill, do not commit adultery, do not steal.' Is there jealousy among you? Do you have an evil inclination?" The angels immediately agreed with G-d...

41. The full phrase reads, "[He] has given us the Torah of truth *and implanted eternal life within us*" (liturgy, *Uva L'tziyon*; blessing recited at the conclusion of an *aliyah* to the Torah). Torah is referred to as "eternal life."

observance of actual *mitzvot* a person fulfills the Supernal intention [of creation], namely, "The Holy One, blessed be He, desired a dwelling place in the lower realms."[42]

And this is [the meaning of the verse], "For *Havaya Elokim* is a sun and a shield": Just as the cloaking of the sun's shield and sheath enables the sun to be tolerated by the earth and its creatures, allowing them to benefit from the sun's light, which is [a manifestation of] the essence of the luminary of the sun,[43] so, too, is this [dynamic] true regarding the two Divine names of *Havaya* and *Elokim*. Creation stems from the name of *Havaya*, but the actualization of creation comes about through the name *Elokim*.[44] This process allows man, by dint of his Divine service, to elicit a revelation from the name of *Havaya* into this physical world. Hence, "At the beginning, darkness," refers to our Divine service within nature to transform the nature into a receptacle for that which transcends nature—which is the aspect of "then light."[45]

*   *   *

"G-D IS ONE": BOTH IN MICROCOSOM AND MACROCOSOM

The Oneness of the Creator can be seen and discerned within all of creation. When a person ponders the world and all that was created, he can perceive the Divine light and vitality that creates and vivifies them.

For it is written, "From my flesh I see G-dliness [*Eloka*]"[46]: A person knows and feels that the critical component of his being is the light and vitality of his soul (and after engaging in

---

42. The discourse has thus established that the purpose of creation is that physical man overcome his many challenges and lead a Torah-true life, thereby making the world an abode for G-d. This is only possible with the creation of physical beings.

43. "Light is like the luminary" (*Iggeret Hakodesh* 20). Although the light yielded by the sun's shield is in-

significant in the face of the powerful sun, it nonetheless directly reflects its luminous source. The same is true of creation: Although *Elokim* yields a Divine light that is greatly "diminished," one can discern how this light in fact reflects the "luminary" of *Havaya*, as will be explained shortly (in both man and creation).

44. The power of creation stems from

מַשְׁלִים הַכַּוָּנָה הָעֶלְיוֹנָה דְּנִתְאַוָּוה הַקָּדוֹשׁ בָּרוּךְ הוּא לִהְיוֹת לוֹ יִתְבָּרֵךְ דִּירָה בַּתַּחְתּוֹנִים.

וְזֶהוּ כִּי שֶׁמֶשׁ וּמָגֵן הוי׳ אֱלֹקִים כְּמוֹ בְּהַשֶּׁמֶשׁ וְהַמָּגֵן דְּעַל יְדֵי כִּסּוּי הַמָּגֵן וְנַרְתֵּק הַשֶּׁמֶשׁ יוּכַל לְהִתְקַבֵּל בָּעוֹלָם וְהַנִּבְרָאִים וְנֶהֱנִים מֵאוֹרוֹ שֶׁהוּא עֶצֶם מְאוֹר הַשֶּׁמֶשׁ כְּמוֹ כֵן הוּא בְּהַב׳ שֵׁמוֹת שֵׁם אֱלֹקִים וְשֵׁם הוי׳. דְּהַהִתְהַוּוּת הוּא מִשֵּׁם הוי׳ רַק שֶׁהַהִתְהַוּוּת בְּפוֹעַל הוּא עַל יְדֵי שֵׁם אֱלֹקִים בִּכְדֵי שֶׁהָאָדָם עַל יְדֵי עֲבוֹדָתוֹ יַמְשִׁיךְ גִּלּוּי שֵׁם הוי׳ בָּאָרֶץ הַלָּזוּ הַגַּשְׁמִית. וְזֶהוּ בְּרֵישָׁא חֲשׁוֹכָא שֶׁהִיא הָעֲבוֹדָה בְּהַטֶּבַע לַעֲשׂוֹת הַטֶּבַע כְּלִי לְמַעְלָה מֵהַטֶּבַע שֶׁהוּא עִנְיָן וְהַדָר נְהוֹרָא.

*   *   *

וְהִנֵּה אַחְדוּת הַבּוֹרֵא יִתְבָּרֵךְ הוּא נִרְאֶה וְנִכָּר בְּכָל הַנִּבְרָאִים וְהַיְינוּ כַּאֲשֶׁר הָאָדָם מִתְבּוֹנֵן בָּעוֹלָם וְהַנִּבְרָאִים הוּא רוֹאֶה הָאוֹר וְהַחַיּוּת הָאֱלֹקִי דְּזֶהוּ מַה שֶּׁמְהַוֶּוה וּמְחַיֶּה הָעוֹלָם וְהַנִּבְרָאִים,

דְּהִנֵּה כְּתִיב מִבְּשָׂרִי אֶחֱזֶה אֱלֹקָה, וּכְמוֹ שֶׁהָאָדָם יוֹדֵעַ וּמַרְגִּישׁ בְּעַצְמוֹ שֶׁהָעִיקָר הוּא בּוֹ אוֹר וְחַיּוּת הַנֶּפֶשׁ (וְעַל יְדֵי

Havaya. But *Elokim* allows for the creation of physical, "independent" beings—creatures that do not naturally sense their spiritual source.

45. When man performs his Divine service amidst the spiritual darkness of our physical world, he is demonstrating that creation is not in fact independent of G-d, but rather a vital part of G-d's supernal design. He therefore replaces the "darkness" with Divine light.

46. Job 19:26. Contextually, the word *Eloka* is translated as "judgment." Thus, the verse would read, "From my flesh I see *judgment*." (See *Rashi* there.) Homiletically, however, the word is translated literally ("G-dliness"), giving support to the idea of learning about G-d's interaction with the world by observing our soul's interaction with our body.

Divine service, he can sense that this vitality is
G-dliness[47])—for in and of itself, the body is insignificant, the
proof being that after the soul departs, although the body may
be perfectly intact, the eye cannot see and the mouth cannot
speak. Thus, it is his vitality that is of consequence.

And just as this is the case with the person, so, too, under-
standably, is it true concerning the world as a whole. The
main ingredient is the Divine light and vitality that vivifies
the world and creation. As stated in *Avot d'Rabbi Nattan*,[48]
man is a miniature world, and the world, a large body. And
just as the critical component in the microcosm is the light
and vitality, the same holds true concerning the macrocosm.

This is the import of *Havaya Echad* ("*Havaya* is One"):
Empirically, we can perceive and see the Oneness of the
blessed Creator in all of creation, as elucidated elsewhere at
length.[49]

This is what prolonging the pronunciation of *Echad*
means: prolonging one's protracted meditation on [the meaning implicit in the words] *Havaya Echad*. Even though this
knowledge is gleaned from intense intellectual analysis, concerning which it says, "Can you by searching find G-d?"[50],
nonetheless, in their soul's understanding,[51] all Jews perceive
this [Oneness].

PROLONGING = PERCEIVING

Prolonging the *Echad* entails contemplating G-d's specific
providence over every aspect of creation, "For He—blessed be
He—provides nourishment and sustenance for all."[52]

---

47. It is apparent that there is some
sort of "life-force" that enlivens the
body; otherwise, what difference is
there between a live body and one
that is not alive? In a deeper sense,
Chasidus explains that this animating
force is in fact a G-dly vitality. It is
G-dliness that vivifies all of creation.
One attains this realization through

Divine service.

48. Chapter 31. *Avot d'Rabbi Nattan*
is a commentary on *Avot* by the Talmudic sage, R. Nattan of Babylonia
(authored c. 121 CE). It is printed in
the standard editions of the Talmud,
usually at the end of the Tractates of
Nezikin.

עֲבוֹדָה הוּא מַרְגִּישׁ שֶׁהַחַיּוּת הוּא אֱלֹקוּת) דְּהַגּוּף בְּעַצְמוֹ אֵינוֹ
דָבָר כְּלָל וְהָרְאָיָה דִּבְצֵאת הַנֶּפֶשׁ מֵהַגּוּף הֲגַם שֶׁיֶּשְׁנָם כָּל
הָאֵבָרִים בִּשְׁלֵימוּת וּמִכָּל מָקוֹם אֵין הָעַיִן רוֹאָה וְאֵין הַפֶּה
יָכוֹל לְדַבֵּר וְכוּ' הֲרֵי הָעִיקָר בּוֹ הוּא חַיּוּתוֹ,

וּכְמוֹ שֶׁהוּא בְּהָאָדָם הִנֵּה מִזֶּה יָבִין גַּם בָּעוֹלָם שֶׁהָעִיקָר
הוּא הָאוֹר וְהַחַיּוּת הָאֱלֹקִי הַמְחַיֶּה אֶת הָעוֹלָם וְהַנִּבְרָאִים
וְכִדְאִיתָא בְּאָבוֹת דְּרַבִּי נָתָן דְּהָאָדָם הוּא עוֹלָם קָטָן וְהָעוֹלָם
הוּא גּוּף גָּדוֹל, וּכְשֵׁם שֶׁבְּהָעוֹלָם קָטָן הֲרֵי הָעִיקָר הוּא הָאוֹר
וְהַחַיּוּת הִנֵּה כְּמוֹ כֵן הוּא בְּהַגּוּף גָּדוֹל,

וְזֶהוּ הוי' אֶחָד דְּאַחְדוּת הַבּוֹרֵא יִתְבָּרֵךְ הוּא נִיכָּר וְנִרְאֶה
בְּמוּחָשׁ בְּכָל הַנִּבְרָאִים, כְּמוֹ שֶׁכָּתוּב בַּאֲרוּכָה בְּמָקוֹם אַחֵר
בְּעִנְיָן זֶה.

וְזֶהוּ כָּל הַמַּאֲרִיךְ בְּאֶחָד שֶׁהוּא לְהַאֲרִיךְ בַּאֲרִיכוּת
הַהִתְבּוֹנְנוּת דַּהוי' אֶחָד דְּעַם הֱיוֹת דִּידִיעָה זוֹ הִיא הֲבָנָה
שִׂכְלִית עִיּוּנִית כְּמוֹ שֶׁכָּתוּב הַחֵקֶר אֱלֹקַהּ תִּמְצָא, אָבֶּער אֵין
נְשָׁמָה הַשָּׂגָה דֶּער הֶערְט זִיךְ דָאס בָּא אַלֶע אִידֶען.

וְזֶהוּ הָאֲרִיכוּת בְּאֶחָד לְהִתְבּוֹנֵן בְּכָל פְּרָטֵי הַנִּבְרָאִים
בְּעִנְיָן הַהַשְׁגָּחָה פְּרָטִית כִּי הוּא יִתְבָּרֵךְ זָן וּמְפַרְנֵס לַכֹּל.

---

49. *Likkutei Torah, Va'etchanan* 4a
ff.; *Derech Mitzvotecha* 45a; *Sefer Ha-maamarim 5657*, p. 48a ff.
This reference apparently applies
to the general subject matter dis-
cussed here. This last phrase, however
—that the Oneness of the Creator
can be discerned in all of creation—
seems to be unique to our discourse.

50. Job 11:7. The literal interpretation of the verse is that one cannot understand G-d's ways in reward
and punishment (*Metzudat David*).
Chasidus interprets the verse that one
cannot "find G-d" through intellectual pursuits (*Tanya*, ch. 2).

51. I.e., the soul's pure intellect, as it
is unencumbered by the restrictions
of a physical brain.

52. From the Blessing After Meals.
Meditating upon G-d's absolute One-

The verse states, "The eyes of all look expectantly to You, and You give them their food at the proper time"[53]—"at the proper time" of the food,[54] as determined by Divine providence. Hence, a person sees clearly that all of his various business maneuverings are of no avail.[55] Therefore, a person's only task is to anticipate G-d's kindness. This requires only that man make a conduit [for G-d's kindness],[56] and then "G-d's blessing will bring riches."[57] Consequently, he needs to make time for communal prayer, and allocate fixed times for Torah-study. This is the meaning of, "[You give them their food] at the proper time": [man receives his sustenance] in the moment decided upon by the Holy One, blessed be He—not [necessarily] in the moment the person wants.

It is written, "Six days you shall labor, and perform all your work."[58] True, work must be performed. However, the work is only a vessel for the Supernal blessing. And in order for the blessing to rest on this vessel, not only must the vessel be pure of deceit, etc., but moreover his means of earning a livelihood must be a proper one according to Torah standards. Then his work will serve as a suitable medium to receive G-d's blessings.

* * *

OPENING STATEMENT REVISITED

Prolonging *Echad* thus denotes focusing on the Oneness of the blessed Creator, in whatever a person sees, both in terms of the Divine Providence extended over himself—how the Holy One, blessed be He, provides his livelihood and watches over him—and in terms of the Divine Providence extended over the Community of Israel, "a single sheep among seventy wolves, and it is safeguarded."[59] Like the saying, "And not just

---

ness within creation—that G-d is the vitality of all existence—leads to the realization that G-d is the true and only source of nourishment and sustenance.

53. Psalms 145:15.

54. Man will only be granted sustenance from on High when the time is ripe for that specific sustenance to be given to him. Hence, as the discourse continues, man's business maneuvers are of no avail to elicit more than what has been allotted to him.

דִּכְתִיב עֵינַי כָּל אֵלֶיךָ יְשַׂבֵּרוּ וְאַתָּה נוֹתֵן לָהֶם אֶת אָכְלָם בְּעִתּוֹ שֶׁל מַאֲכָל כְּפִי שֶׁהוּקְצַב מֵהַהַשְׁגָּחָה הָעֶלְיוֹנָה וְכֵן רוֹאֶה הָאָדָם בְּמוּחָשׁ דְּכָל תַּחְבּוּלוֹתָיו בְּעֵסֶק מַשָּׂא וּמַתָּן הֵם לִבְלִי הוֹעִיל, וְעַל כֵּן הִנֵּה כָּל עֲבוֹדַת הָאָדָם הוּא רַק לְצַפּוֹת לְחַסְדּוֹ יִתְבָּרֵךְ דְּאֵינוֹ צָרִיךְ אֶלָּא לַעֲשׂוֹת כְּלִי וּבִרְכַּת הוי׳ הִיא תַעֲשִׁיר, וּבְמֵילָא צָרִיךְ לִהְיוֹת לוֹ זְמַן עַל תְּפִלָּה בְּצִבּוּר וּקְבִיעוּת עִתִּים לַתּוֹרָה דְּזֶהוּ וְאַתָּה נוֹתֵן לָהֶם אֶת אָכְלָם בְּעִתּוֹ, בְּעִתּוֹ שֶׁל הַקָּדוֹשׁ בָּרוּךְ הוּא וְלֹא בְּעֵת שֶׁהָאָדָם רוֹצֶה,

וּכְתִיב שֵׁשֶׁת יָמִים תַּעֲבוֹד וְעָשִׂיתָ כָּל מְלַאכְתֶּךָ שֶׁצְּרִיכִים עֲשִׂיַּית מְלָאכָה, אָמְנָם אֵינוֹ אֶלָּא רַק כְּלִי לְבִרְכָה הָעֶלְיוֹנָה וּבִכְדֵי שֶׁתִּשְׁרֶה בָּהּ הַבְּרָכָה הִנֵּה לֹא זוֹ בִּלְבָד שֶׁצְּרִיכָה לִהְיוֹת כְּלִי טָהוֹרָה מִגְּנֵיבַת דַּעַת וְכוּ׳ אֶלָּא עוֹד זֹאת שֶׁתִּהְיֶה כְּלִי פַּרְנָסָתוֹ כְּשֵׁרָה עַל פִּי הַתּוֹרָה, וְאָז הוּא כְּלִי לְבִרְכַּת הוי׳.

* * *

וְזֶהוּ כָּל הַמַּאֲרִיךְ בְּאֶחָד שֶׁצְּרִיכִים לְהַאֲרִיךְ בְּאֶחָד הַיְינוּ שֶׁבְּכָל דָּבָר וְדָבָר שֶׁהָאָדָם רוֹאֶה יָשִׂים אֶל לִבּוֹ אַחְדוּת הַבּוֹרֵא יִתְבָּרֵךְ הֵן מַה שֶׁהָאָדָם רוֹאֶה בְּעַצְמוֹ הַהַשְׁגָּחָה הָעֶלְיוֹנָה בְּהַנּוֹגֵעַ לְעַצְמוֹ שֶׁהַקָּדוֹשׁ בָּרוּךְ הוּא מַזְמִין לוֹ פַּרְנָסָתוֹ וְשׁוֹמֵר אוֹתוֹ כוּ׳ כֵּן הוּא הַהַשְׁגָּחָה פְּרָטִית בִּכְלַל יִשְׂרָאֵל וּכְמַאֲמָר כְּבִשָׂה אַחַת בֵּין ע׳ זְאֵבִים וְהִיא מִשְׁתַּמֶּרֶת, וּכְמַאֲמָר וְלֹא אֶחָד

---

55. Overindulging in business schemes can only cause harm, since it will divert one's energy away from G-d, the true source of his blessing. See *The Unbreakable Soul*, p. 20 ff. (Kehot 2003).

56. The discourse proceeds to explain how one makes this conduit.

57. Proverbs 10:22.

58. Exodus 20:9.

59. See *Petikta Rabbati* 9:2; *Tanchuma*, *Toldot* 5; *Esther Rabbah* 10:11.

one alone has risen against us…and the Holy One, blessed be He, saves us from their hands."[60] Accordingly, one has to fortify one's worship of G-d by participating in communal prayer and by scheduling fixed times for Torah study.[61]

Hence, Rav Acha bar Yaakov remarks that the *dalet* of *Echad* is prolonged. The *dalet* alludes to the four directions[62] of the world. Every individual has to realize that Torah and *mitzvot* are eternal, applicable at all times, and in all places.[63] A person cannot claim that his environment is responsible—that in certain countries, observing *mitzvot* is possible, while in other countries, it is not. Heaven forefend to say such a thing!

On the verse "For I have spread you as the four directions of the heavens,"[64] our Sages comment: "Just as it is impossible for the world to exist without its four directions, so is it impossible for the world to exist without the Jewish people."[65] "G-d guides the footsteps of man"[66] in the direction that will lead to the fulfillment of the Divine intent of desiring a dwelling place in the lower realms, through our service in Torah and *mitzvot*.[67] This is the meaning of protracting *Echad* by prolonging the enunciation of the *dalet*: it indicates that this [spiritual service] applies to every country equally.[68]

PRECEDING BERAITA REVISITED

This is [the meaning of] *Our Sages taught: Hear O Israel, Havaya is our G-d (Elokeinu), Havaya is One (Echad):*

Hear O Israel—a Jew perceives that *Havaya Elokeinu* —that our power and life-force comes from the name of

---

60. Haggadah for Pesach, *V'hi She'amda*.

61. When one recognizes that the life-force of all of creation stems from G-d, who provides for and sustains each individual in particular and the entire Jewish nation as a whole, he will focus his attention toward the Source of his blessing and strengthen

his commitment to communal prayer and Torah study.

62. I.e., "corners."

63. Torah and *mitzvot* are relevant in all four directions of the world—*dalet*.

64. Zechariah 2:10.

בִּלְבָד עָמַד עָלֵינוּ כו' וְהַקָּדוֹשׁ בָּרוּךְ הוּא מַצִּילֵנוּ מִיָּדָם עַל כֵּן צָרִיךְ לְהִתְחַזֵּק בַּעֲבוֹדַת ה' בִּתְפִלָּה בְּצִבּוּר וּבִקְבִיעוֹת עִתִּים לַתּוֹרָה,

וְזֶהוּ דְּאָמַר רַבִּי אַחָא בַּר יַעֲקֹב שֶׁצְּרִיכִים לְהַאֲרִיךְ בְּהַד' דְּאֶחָד, דְּהַד' הוּא ד' רוּחוֹת הָעוֹלָם שֶׁכָּל אָדָם צָרִיךְ לָדַעַת דְּהַתּוֹרָה וּמִצְוֹת נִצְחִים הֵמָּה בְּכָל זְמַן וּבְכָל מָקוֹם וְאַל יֹאמַר הָאוֹמֵר כִּי הַמָּקוֹם גּוֹרֵם שֶׁבִּמְדִינָה זוֹ אֶפְשָׁר לְקַיֵּים תּוֹרָה וּמִצְוֹת וּבִמְדִינָה אַחֶרֶת אִי אֶפְשָׁר, חַס וְשָׁלוֹם לֵאמֹר כֵּן,

דְּהִנֵּה כְּתִיב כִּי כְּאַרְבַּע רוּחוֹת הַשָּׁמַיִם פֵּרַשְׂתִּי אֶתְכֶם וְאָמְרוּ רַבּוֹתֵינוּ זִכְרוֹנָם לִבְרָכָה כְּשֵׁם שֶׁאִי אֶפְשָׁר לָעוֹלָם בְּלִי רוּחוֹת כַּךְ אִי אֶפְשָׁר לָעוֹלָם בְּלִי יִשְׂרָאֵל, דְּמֵה' מִצְעֲדֵי גֶבֶר כּוֹנָנוּ לְהַשְׁלִים הַכַּוָּונָה הָעֶלְיוֹנָה דְּנִתְאַוֶּוה הַקָּדוֹשׁ בָּרוּךְ הוּא לִהְיוֹת לוֹ יִתְבָּרֵךְ דִּירָה בַּתַּחְתּוֹנִים עַל יְדֵי עֲבוֹדָתָם בַּתּוֹרָה וּמִצְוֹת וְזֶהוּ דַּאֲרִיכוּת הָאֶחָד הוּא בְּהַד' הַיְינוּ בְּכָל מְדִינָה וּמְדִינָה בְּשָׁוֶה.

וְזֶהוּ תָּנוּ רַבָּנָן שְׁמַע יִשְׂרָאֵל הוי' אֱלֵקֵינוּ הוי' אֶחָד,

דְּשְׁמַע יִשְׂרָאֵל אַ אִיד דֶּער הֶערְט דַּהוי' אֱלֵקֵינוּ, אַז אוּנְזֶער כֹּחַ אוּן חַיּוּת אִיז פוּן שֵׁם הוי' וָואס אִיז הֶעכֶער פוּן

---

65. *Taanit* 3b; *Zohar* II:4b.

66. Psalms 37:23.

67. Thus, not only are the Jewish people as vital to the world's existence as the "four directions," since they fulfill G-d's purpose in creation (as the Talmud's interpretation of the verse), their task also occurs *through-*

out the "four directions"—throughout the entire world, in every country, without exception (as the verse's literal meaning).

68. The *dalet* ("four") is prolonged to emphasize that all *four* directions of the world are equal with regards to the practice of Judaism.

Havaya, which transcends the [element of] nature that comes from the name *Elokim.*[69] And this knowledge results from the soul's understanding[70] of *Havaya Echad*—G-d's Oneness.[71]

R. Meir remarks, *Until here, concentration of the heart is required*: Although this knowledge and recognition of G-d's Oneness [initially] engages [only] the mind, nonetheless, each and every Jew has the ability to inculcate this intellectual realization into the heart. This is in consonance with the teaching, "An oath is administered [to the soul before its descent]: *Be righteous*."[72] For how is it possible to make the soul responsible for the righteousness of the body?[73] Rather the explanation of this teaching is that this oath implies satiation.[74] The soul is satiated with the power necessary to vanquish the body and the natural soul, to purify and refine it, and thereby make it into a vessel that can contain the revelation of the Divine light.

* * *

So R. Meir remarks that *Until here, concentration of the heart is required*—that this knowledge should not remain relegated to the mind, but should lead to "concentration of the heart," so as to develop actual fine character-traits.[75]

Hence, **Whoever** *prolongs the Echad*: Every individual is to *prolong the Echad*—[i.e., extend his recognition of] the Oneness of G-d, according to his ability. And the focus is on the *dalet*. A person should know that he must engage in the study of Torah and in Divine service wherever he may be. And everyone is obligated in the study of Torah;[76] even a person who is harried and extremely distracted must schedule fixed times for Torah study. Simple folk, too, who cannot study themselves, are obligated to attend public classes.

---

69. See p. 24.

70. See footnote 51.

71. See p. 26 and footnotes 16 and 17.

72. *Niddah* 30b.

73. Soul and body are two opposites: the soul desires G-dliness, the body desires physicality. How, then, can the soul accept responsibility for the body?

דֶער טֶבַע וּוָאס עַל יְדֵי שֵׁם אֱלֹקִים, אוּן דֶער דֶערְהֶער קוּמְט
פוּן דֶער נְשָׁמָה פַארְשְׁטַאנְד אִין הוי׳ אֶחָד הַיְינוּ אַחְדוּת
הַבּוֹרֵא יִתְבָּרֵךְ.

וְאָמַר רַבִּי מֵאִיר עַד כַּאן צְרִיכִים כַּוָּונַת הַלֵּב, דְּהַגַּם
דִּידִיעָה וְהַשָּׂגָה זוֹ דַהוי׳ אֶחָד הִיא כַּוָּונַת הַמּוֹחַ אֲבָל כָּל אֶחָד
מִיִּשְׂרָאֵל בִּיכוֹלְתּוֹ לְהָבִיא הַשָּׂגָה זוֹ מֵהַמּוֹחַ אֶל הַלֵּב וּכְמַאֲמַר
מַשְׁבִּיעִין אוֹתוֹ תְּהֵא צַדִּיק, דְּלִכְאוֹרָה אֵיךְ אֶפְשָׁר לְהַשְׁבִּיעַ אֶת
הַנְּשָׁמָה שֶׁהַגּוּף יִהְיֶה צַדִּיק אֶלָּא הַפֵּירוּשׁ מַשְׁבִּיעִין אוֹתוֹ תְּהֵא
צַדִּיק דְּבִשְׁבוּעָה זוֹ פֵּירוּשָׁהּ שׂוֹבַע שֶׁנוֹתְנִים כֹּחַ וְשׂוֹבַע
לְהַנְּשָׁמָה שֶׁתּוּכַל לְהִתְגַּבֵּר עַל הַגּוּף וְנֶפֶשׁ הַטִבְעִי לְבָרְרוֹ
וּלְזַכְּכוֹ וְלַעֲשׂוֹתוֹ כְּלִי לְאוֹר הָאֱלֹקִי בְּגִילוּי.

* * *

וְאָמַר רַבִּי מֵאִיר דְּעַד כַּאן צְרִיכִים כַּוָּונַת הַלֵּב, הַיְינוּ
דִּידִיעָה זוֹ לֹא תִּשָּׁאֵר רַק בַּמּוֹחַ כִּי אִם יָבִיא אוֹתָהּ בְּכַוָּונַת
הַלֵּב עַל מְנָת לַהֲבִיאָהּ בְּמִדּוֹת טוֹבוֹת בְּפוֹעַל מַמָּשׁ.

וְזֶהוּ כָּל הַמַּאֲרִיךְ בְּאֶחָד דְּכָל אֶחָד וְאֶחָד לְפִי כֹחוֹ צָרִיךְ
לְהַאֲרִיךְ בְּאֶחָד, וְהַיְינוּ בְּאַחְדוּת הוי׳ וְהָעִיקָר הוּא בְּהַד׳
שֶׁיֵּדַע הָאָדָם דְּבְכָל מָקוֹם שֶׁהוּא צָרִיךְ לַעֲסוֹק בְּתוֹרָה
וַעֲבוֹדָה, וְהַכֹּל חַיָּיבִים בְּתַלְמוּד תּוֹרָה, אֲפִילוּ מִי שֶׁהוּא טָרוּד
וּמוּטְרָד בְּיוֹתֵר צָרִיךְ לִקְבּוֹעַ עִתִּים לַתּוֹרָה, וַאֲפִילוּ אֲנָשִׁים
פְּשׁוּטִים שֶׁאֵינָם יְכוֹלִים לִלְמוֹד בְּעַצְמָם צְרִיכִים לִשְׁמוֹעַ מִפִּי
הַמְלַמֵּד בָּרַבִּים.

---

74. The Hebrew word for oath, *sh'vuah*, is of the same root as *sovah*, satiation [שבע]. The letters of *shin* and *sin* are interchangeable with each other.

75. See p. 22.

76. *Rambam, Hilchot Talmud Torah* 1:8; *Shulchan Aruch, Yorah De'ah* 246:1; Rabbi Schneur Zalman of Liadi, *Hilchot Talmud Torah* 1:4, 2:1.

This, then, is the meaning of Rav Acha bar Yaakov's statement: *And that is the dalet*—that the prolongation of the word *Echad* lies primarily in the *dalet*.[77] Some people are mistaken in this respect, and to excuse their laxity, they devise absurd rationalizations.[78]

And Rav Ashi said: *Provided that he does not hurry the* [pronunciation of the letter] *chet*. The *chet* [whose numerical value is eight] alludes to the seven firmaments[79] and to earth. A person should take to heart that the soul descends into the body to fulfill the purpose [of creation], that "G-d desired an abode in the lower realms." This is the idea of the seven firmaments and earth: The soul's descent from the seven firmaments to earth, to be vested within a physical body, is for the subsequent ascent[80] that occurs when man engages in the study of Torah and the observance of *mitzvot* on this physical earth.[81]

On the verse, "Is not man on earth for a limited time, and are his days [not] like the days of a hired worker?"[82], *Rashi*

---

77. Every person, no matter where he may be (*dalet*), must recognize the Oneness of G-d (*Echad*) and engage in Torah study, prayer and the fulfillment of *mitzvot*.

78. Such as those who said at the time "America is different"—that the "customs" of the old country are not applicable in today's modern American society. See *Sefer Hasichot 5703*, p. 147; *Sefer Hasichot 5705*, p. 77.

79. SEVEN FIRMAMENTS. These are seven spiritual realms, one above the other. See *Chagigah* 12b: Rabbi Yehudah said, "There are two heavens, as it is written, 'The heaven, the heaven of heaven, the earth and everything in it, all belong to G-d' (Deuteronomy 10:14)." Reish Lakish maintained there are seven heavens, namely: *Vilon* ("Curtain"), *Rakiya* ("Sky"), *Sh'chakim*

("Mills"), *Z'vul* ("Residence"), *Ma'on* ("Abode"), *Machon* ("Arsenal") and *Aravot* ("Plains" or "Wide Spaces").

Reish Lakish enumerated: *Vilon* serves no purpose. *Rakiya* contains the sun, moon, stars, zodiac and all the Heavenly Hosts. In *Sh'chakim*, the mills grind manna for the Righteous for the World to Come. *Z'vul* contains an altar upon which the angel Michael, the great minister, offers sacrifices. In *Ma'on*, groups of angels chant song. *Machon* contains storages of snow and hail. *Aravot* contains righteousness and justice, the vaults of life and peace and the vaults of blessing, the souls of the righteous, spirits and souls to be born in the future and the dew with which G-d will resurrect the dead.

(*Kesef Mishnah* (*Yesodei Hatorah* 3:1) explains that Rabbi Yehudah and Reish Lakish do not disagree; rather,

וְזֶהוּ שֶׁאָמַר רַבִּי אַחָא בַּר יַעֲקֹב וּבְדַלֵּית, דְּהָאֲרִיכוּת בְּאֶחָד הָעִיקָר הוּא בְּהַד׳. דִּלְפִי שֶׁיֵּשׁ טוֹעִים בָּזֶה וּמְקִילִים לְעַצְמָם בִּטְעָנוֹת שֶׁל הֶבֶל.

וְאָמַר רַב אַשִׁי שֶׁלֹּא יַחְטוֹף בַּחֵי״ת. דְּכַוָּנַת הַחֵי״ת הוּא ז׳ רְקִיעִים וָאָרֶץ וְהַיְינוּ שֶׁהָאָדָם יִתֵּן אֶל לִבּוֹ דִּירִידַת הַנְּשָׁמָה בַּגּוּף הִיא בִּשְׁבִיל הַכַּוָּונָה דְּנִתְאַוָּוה הַקָּדוֹשׁ בָּרוּךְ הוּא לִהְיוֹת לוֹ יִתְבָּרֵךְ דִּירָה בַּתַּחְתּוֹנִים דְּזֶהוּ הַז׳ רְקִיעִים וָאָרֶץ דְּמַה שֶׁהַנְּשָׁמָה יוֹרֶדֶת מֵהַז׳ רְקִיעִים לָאָרֶץ הַלֵּזוּ לְהִתְלַבֵּשׁ בְּגוּף גַּשְׁמִי הִנֵּה יְרִידָה זוֹ הִיא בִּשְׁבִיל הָעֲלִיָּה שֶׁתִּהְיֶה עַל יְדֵי שֶׁהָאָדָם יִתְעַסֵּק בְּלִימּוּד הַתּוֹרָה וְקִיּוּם הַמִּצְוֹת בָּאָרֶץ הַלֵּזוּ הַגַּשְׁמִית.

וּכְתִיב הֲלֹא צָבָא לֶאֱנוֹשׁ עֲלֵי אָרֶץ וְכִימֵי שָׂכִיר יָמָיו. וּפֵרֵשׁ רַשִׁ״י כְּמוֹ הַשָּׂכִיר הַזֶּה שֶׁנִּשְׂכַּר לְשָׁנָה וְיוֹדֵעַ שֶׁיִּכְלֶה

Rabbi Yehudah counts only the visible heavens (the *Shamayim*) containing the sun, moon and stars, whereas Reish Lakish also counts the celestial spheres—which are loftier than *Shamayim*—and calls them all *Shamayim*.)

80. Chasidus describes different aspects of the "ascent" that occurs through the soul's descent into this world. Among them:

1. Prior to its descent, the soul is in a spiritual paradise, unchallenged in its spiritual service. When the soul descends below, however, it is met constantly with opposition from the body and the "animal soul," who wish only to pursue material interests. When the soul overcomes this challenge and fulfills its spiritual calling, it expresses

its unwavering devotion to G-d, even in the face of adversity —something that cannot be recognized when the soul is in its spiritual oasis above.

2. It is only after its descent that the soul can *practically* fulfill Torah and *mitzvot*, and thereby gain their spiritual benefit.

3. Only through its spiritual service on this world can the soul fulfill G-d's purpose of creation—that the world be an abode for His presence.

For further discussion of this topic see *Likkutei Sichot*, vol. 15, p. 245 ff.

81. This adds even more import to one's spiritual service, knowing that it was for this that his soul descended in the first place.

82. Job 7:1.

comments that just like a hired worker—contracted for a year—realizes that his time will eventually run out, similarly every person should consider that he too was given an allotted time, a certain number of years to live in this world. The days and years of each and every person is measured, as it says, "Days have been formed."[83]

It is also written, "[You shall therefore, observe the commandments, the statutes, and the ordinances, which I command you] *this day to do them.*"[84] Torah study—to know how to act—and practical mitzvah observance are possible only in *this* world.[85] And it was to this end that the soul descended below.

Thus, *Provided that he does not hurry the chet*: A man must not forget the truth as to why he came into the world.[86] And if he is genuinely engrossed [in this truth] then he will automatically prolong the *dalet*; [i.e.,] wherever he finds himself, he will study the Torah and observe its *mitzvot*. And *Whoever prolongs the Echad*—meaning, whoever devotes and dedicates himself to extend the Oneness [of G-d] by publicizing G-d in the world—*has his days and years prolonged*. The Holy One, blessed be He, grants the person longevity, with years of goodness illuminated by the light of Torah and Divine service, so that he will succeed in his Divine service—in order to accomplish the true intent [of creation], to make a dwelling place for G-d in this world.

* * *

May the Almighty grant us all—among all of Israel—long life, [enabling us] to disseminate the teachings of Torah and its study, and [to attract people to be] involved in "service of the heart"—prayer, so that we merit to achieve G-d's objective, [doing so] with an abundance of everything good materially and spiritually.

---

83. Psalms 139:16. I.e., a specific amount of days are created for each individual.

84. Deuteronomy 7:11.

85. As opposed to the spiritual realms; see *Likkutei Torah, Va'etchanan* 6b. One can only study the practical application of Torah and fulfill the *mitzvot* in this physical world, a

זְמַנּוּ כֵּן הָאָדָם צָרִיךְ לָשׂוּם לְבּוֹ שֶׁנִּיתַּן לוֹ זְמַן קָצוּב כַּמָּה שָׁנִים יִחְיֶה בְּעוֹלָם זֶה. וּכְתִיב יָמִים יוּצָרוּ כו׳ דְּכָל אֶחָד וְאֶחָד יָמָיו וּשְׁנוֹתָיו הֵם מְדוּדִים,

וּכְתִיב הַיּוֹם לַעֲשׂוֹתָם, דְּלִימּוּד הַתּוֹרָה לְמַעַן לֵידַע אֶת הַמַּעֲשֶׂה אֲשֶׁר יַעֲשׂוּן וְקִיּוּם הַמִּצְוֹת מַעֲשִׂיּוֹת הֵם בָּעוֹלָם הַזֶּה דַּוְקָא. וּבִשְׁבִיל זֶה הָיְתָה יְרִידַת הַנְּשָׁמָה לְמַטָּה,

וְזֶהוּ שֶׁלֹּא יַחֲטוֹף בַּחֵית, דֶּער מֶענְטְשׁ זָאהְל נִיט פַארְגֶעסְסְען אוֹיפֶּען אֶמֶת צוּלִיעָב דֶעם וָואס עֶר אִיז גֶעקוּמֶען אוֹיף דֶער וֶועלְט. אוּן אַז עֶר וֶועט לִיגֶען אִין דֶעם מִיט אֵיין אֶמֶת הִנֵּה בְּמֵילָא יַאֲרִיךְ בְּהַד׳, הַיְינוּ דְּבְכָל מָקוֹם שֶׁהוּא נִמְצָא יִתְעַסֵּק בַּתּוֹרָה וְקִיּוּם הַמִּצְוֹת, וְכָל הַמַּאֲרִיךְ בְּאֶחָד הַיְינוּ שֶׁמּוֹסֵר וְנוֹתֵן עַצְמוֹ לְהַאֲרִיךְ בְּאֶחָד לְפַרְסֵם אֱלֹקוּתוֹ יִתְבָּרֵךְ בָּעוֹלָם הִנֵּה מַאֲרִיכִין לוֹ יָמָיו וּשְׁנוֹתָיו שֶׁהַקָּדוֹשׁ בָּרוּךְ הוּא נוֹתֵן לְהָאָדָם אֲרִיכוּת יָמִים וְשָׁנִים טוֹבוֹת וּמְאִירוֹת בְּאוֹר תּוֹרָה וַעֲבוֹדָה, לְהַצְלִיחוֹ בַּעֲבוֹדָתוֹ, בִּכְדֵי לְהַשְׁלִים הַכַּוָּנָה הָאֲמִיתִית לַעֲשׂוֹת לוֹ יִתְבָּרֵךְ דִּירָה בַּתַּחְתּוֹנִים.

*   *   *

וְהַשֵּׁם יִתְבָּרֵךְ יִתֵּן לָנוּ וְלָכֶם בְּתוֹךְ כְּלַל יִשְׂרָאֵל אֲרִיכוּת יָמִים וְשָׁנִים, לִפְעוֹל הַרְבָּצַת הַתּוֹרָה וְלִימּוּדָהּ וְהִתְעַסְּקוּת עֲבוֹדָה שֶׁבַּלֵּב זוֹ תְּפִלָּה בִּשְׁבִיל לִזְכּוֹת לְהַשְׁלִים הַכַּוָּנָה הָעֶלְיוֹנָה בְּרוֹב טוֹב בְּגַשְׁמִיּוּת וְרוּחָנִיּוּת.

---

world upon which man's time is limited. This should further encourage one to refocus on this most urgent of tasks.

Note *Eruvin* 22a: "Rabbi Yehoshua ben Levi said: "What is the meaning of [the verse] *which I command you this day to do them*? ... To-day—to do them, *in the future*—to receive their reward."

86. I.e., to make the world an abode for G-d through learning Torah and fulfilling *mitzvot*. The *chet*, as explained above, alludes to the soul's descent to this world and its purpose.

APPENDIX

APPENDIX[1]

LETTER BY RABBI YOSEF YITZCHAK OF LUBAVITCH

FREE RENDITION

By the Grace of G-d,
3 Iyar 5690
Detroit

To the Jewish people of Chicago,
May G-d bless you.

Greeting and blessing!

Meeting with a large segment of the Jewish population, in various synagogues during my stay in Chicago, made a good impression on me, seeing, as it were, how warm the Jewish heart is.

I hope to G-d that my visit to Chicago will be remembered in every Jewish home, so as to strengthen Torah and Judaism.

I joyfully give my blessing to every Jewish family, that the Almighty, blessed be He, should bless them all with healthy Jewish children, with long and healthy years, and with abundant livelihood.

I remain their friend, who seeks their welfare, honors them and blesses them

Yosef Yitzchak

---

1. This letter originally appeared in Yiddish in the *Chicago Daily Jewish Courier* on 9 May, 1930, and subsequently in Rabbi Yosef Yitzchak's *Igrot Kodesh*, vol. 13, p. 223.

INDEX

INDEX

OTHER TITLES IN
THE CHASIDIC HERITAGE SERIES

THE ETERNAL BOND *from Torah Or*

By Rabbi Schneur Zalman of Liadi
Translated by Rabbi Ari Sollish

This discourse explores the spiritual significance of *brit milah*, analyzing two dimensions in which our connection with G-d may be realized. For in truth, there are two forms of spiritual circumcision: Initially, man must "circumcise his heart," freeing himself to the best of his ability from his negative, physical drives; ultimately, though, it is G-d who truly liberates man from his material attachment.

∽∾∽

JOURNEY OF THE SOUL from *Torah Or*

By Rabbi Schneur Zalman of Liadi
Translated by Rabbi Ari Sollish

Drawing upon the parallel between Queen Esther's impassioned plea to King Ahasuerus for salvation and the soul's entreaty to G-d for help in its spiritual struggle, this discourse examines the root of the soul's exile, and the dynamics by which it lifts itself from the grip of materiality and ultimately finds a voice with which to express its G-dly yearnings. Includes a brief biography of the author.

∽∾∽

TRANSFORMING THE INNER SELF from *Likkutei Torah*

By Rabbi Schneur Zalman of Liadi
Translated by Rabbi Chaim Zev Citron

This discourse presents a modern-day perspective on the Biblical command to offer animal sacrifices. Rabbi Schneur Zalman teaches that each of us possesses certain character traits that can be seen as "animalistic," or materialistic, in nature, which can lead a person toward a life of material indulgence. Our charge, then, is to "sacrifice" and transform the animal within, to refine our animal traits and utilize them in our pursuit of spiritual perfection.

∽∾∽

FLAMES from *Gates of Radiance*
By Rabbi DovBer of Lubavitch
Translated by Dr. Naftoli Loewenthal
This discourse focuses on the multiple images of the lamp, the oil, the wick and the different hues of the flame in order to express profound guidance in the divine service of every individual. Although *Flames* is a Chanukah discourse, at the same time, it presents concepts that are of perennial significance. Includes the first English biography of the author ever published.

᠊ᠥ᠊ᠥ᠊ᠥ

THE MITZVAH TO LOVE YOUR FELLOW AS YOUR-SELF from *Derech Mitzvotecha*
By Rabbi Menachem Mendel of Lubavitch, the Tzemach Tzedek
Translated by Rabbis Nissan Mangel and Zalman I. Posner
The discourse discusses the Kabbalistic principle of the "collective soul of the world of *Tikkun*" and explores the essential unity of all souls. The discourse develops the idea that when we connect on a soul level, we can love our fellow as we love ourselves; for in truth, we are all one soul. Includes a brief biography of the author.

᠊ᠥ᠊ᠥ᠊ᠥ

TRUE EXISTENCE *Mi Chamocha 5629*
By Rabbi Shmuel of Lubavitch
Translated by Rabbis Yosef Marcus and Avraham D. Vaisfiche
This discourse revolutionizes the age-old notion of Monotheism, i.e., that there is no other god besides Him. Culling from Talmudic and Midrashic sources, the discourse makes the case that not only is there no other god besides Him, there is nothing besides Him—literally. The only thing that truly exists is G-d. Includes a brief biography of the author.

᠊ᠥ᠊ᠥ᠊ᠥ

TRUE EXISTENCE *The Chasidic View of Reality*
A Video-CD with Rabbi Manis Friedman
Venture beyond science and Kabbalah and discover the world of Chasidism. This Video-CD takes the viewer step-by-step through the basic chasidic and kabbalistic view of creation and existence. In clear, lucid language, Rabbi Manis Friedman deciphers these esoteric concepts and demonstrates their modern-day applications.

৯৯৯

YOM TOV SHEL ROSH HASHANAH 5659
Discourse One
By Rabbi Shalom DovBer of Lubavitch
Translated by Rabbis Yosef Marcus and Moshe Miller
The discourse explores the attribute of *malchut* and the power of speech while introducing some of the basic concepts of Chasidism and Kabbalah in a relatively easy to follow format. Despite its title and date of inception, the discourse is germane throughout the year. Includes a brief biography of the author.

৯৯৯

FORCES IN CREATION
Yom Tov Shel Rosh Hashanah 5659 Discourse Two
By Rabbi Shalom DovBer of Lubavitch
Translated by Rabbis Moshe Miller and Shmuel Marcus
This is a fascinating journey beyond the terrestrial, into the myriad spiritual realms that shape our existence. In this discourse, Rabbi Shalom DovBer systematically traces the origins of earth, Torah and souls, drawing the reader higher and higher into the mystical, cosmic dimensions that lie beyond the here and now, and granting a deeper awareness of who we are at our core.

৯৯৯

THE POWER OF RETURN
Yom Tov Shel Rosh Hashanah 5659 Discourse Three
By Rabbi Shalom DovBer of Lubavitch
Translated by Rabbi Y. Eliezer Danzinger
In this discourse Rabbi Shalom DovBer examines of the inner workings of *teshuvah*, and explains how it is precisely through making a detailed and honest examination of one's character and spiritual standing—which inevitably leads one to a contrite and broken heart—that allows one to realize his or her essential connection with G-d.

ৰ্কৈৰ্কৈৰ্কৈ

OVERCOMING FOLLY
Kuntres Umaayan Mibeit Hashem
By Rabbi Shalom DovBer of Lubavitch
Translated by Rabbi Zalman I. Posner
In this classis ethico-philosophical work, Rabbi Shalom DovBer weaves Chasidic doctrine, Kabbalah thoughts, Biblical and Talmudic texts and candid insights into human frailties into a document structured and systematic, yet informal and personal—a text for study and meditation.

ৰ্কৈৰ্কৈৰ্কৈ

THE PRINCIPLES OF EDUCATION AND GUIDANCE
Klalei Hachinuch Vehahadrachah
By Rabbi Yosef Yitzchak of Lubavitch
Translated by Rabbi Y. Eliezer Danzinger
The Principles of Education and Guidance is a compelling treatise that examines the art of educating. In this thought provoking analysis, Rabbi Yosef Yitzchak teaches how to assess the potential of any pupil, how to objectively evaluate one's own strengths, and how to successfully use reward and punishment—methods that will help one become a more effective educator.

ৰ্কৈৰ্কৈৰ্কৈ

THE FOUR WORLDS

By Rabbi Yosef Yitzchak of Lubavitch
Translated by Rabbis Yosef Marcus and Avraham D. Vaisfiche
Overview by Rabbi J. Immanuel Schochet

At the core of our identity is the desire to be one with our source, and to know the spiritual realities that give our physical life the transcendental importance of the Torah's imperatives. In this letter to a yearning Chasid, the Rebbe explains the mystical worlds of Atzilut, Beriah, Yetzira, and Asiya.

ONENESS IN CREATION *Kol Hamaarich B'Echad 5690*

By Rabbi Yosef Yitzchak of Lubavitch
Translated by Rabbi Y. Eliezer Danzinger

Said by Rabbi Yosef Yitzchak at the close of his 1930 visit to Chicago, this discourse explores the concept of Divine Unity as expressed in the first verse of the Shema. The discourse maintains that it is a G-dly force that perpetually sustains all of creation. As such, G-d is one with creation. And it is our study of Torah and performance of the mitzvot that reveals this essential oneness.

ക്കക

CREATION AND REDEMPTION *Hachodesh 5700*

By Rabbi Yosef Yitzchak of Lubavitch
Translated by Rabbi Yosef Marcus

Tishrei celebrates Creation, the birth of the world, indicative of the natural order. Nissan commemorates the miraculous Exodus from Egypt, or the supernatural. In human terms, when struggling with the obfuscation of the natural, the key is to recognize the dimension where the limitations of the natural order do not exist. In fact, the physical exists only so that we may demonstrate how it too exposes the Divine truth. And when we recognize this, we can realize the supernatural even within the natural.

ക്കക

GARMENTS OF THE SOUL *Vayishlach Yehoshua 5736*
By Rabbi Menachem M. Schneerson, the Lubavitcher Rebbe
Translated by Rabbi Yosef Marcus

Often what is perceived in this world as secondary is in reality most sublime. What appears to be mundane and inconsequential is often most sacred and crucial. Thus, at their source, the garments of the human, both physical and spiritual, transcend the individual.

❦❦❦

THE UNBREAKABLE SOUL *Mayim Rabbim 5738*
By Rabbi Menachem M. Schneerson, the Lubavitcher Rebbe
Translated by Rabbi Ari Sollish

No matter how much one may be inundated with materialism, the flame of the soul burns forever. A discourse that begins with an unequivocal declaration, it speaks to one who finds pleasure in the material world, yet struggles to find spirituality in his or her life.

❦❦❦

VICTORY OF LIGHT *Tanu Rabanan Mitzvat Ner Chanukah 5738*
By Rabbi Menachem M. Schneerson, the Lubavitcher Rebbe
Translated by Rabbi Yosef Marcus

Even darkness has a purpose: to be transformed into light. This discourse explains how we can draw strength from the story of Chanukah for our battle with spiritual darkness, so that we, like the Macabees of old, may attain a *Victory of Light*.

❦❦❦

ON THE ESSENCE OF CHASIDUS
Kuntres Inyana Shel Toras Hachasidus
By Rabbi Menachem M. Schneerson, the Lubavitcher Rebbe

This landmark discourse explores the contribution of Chasidus to a far deeper and expanded understanding of Torah. The Rebbe analyzes the relationship Chasidus has with Kabbalah, the various dimensions of the soul, the concept of Moshiach and the Divine attributes.

❦❦❦

NURTURING FAITH *Kuntres Purim Kattan 5752*
By Rabbi Menachem M. Schneerson, the Lubavitcher Rebbe
Translated by Rabbi Yosef Marcus

At its core, this discourse discusses the function of a *nassi*, a Jewish leader, who awakens within every single person the deepest part of the soul. Similar to Moses, the *nassi* inspires the person so that one's most basic faith in G-d leaves the realm of the abstract and becomes real. *Nurturing Faith* will cultivate your bond with the Rebbe's role as the Moses of our generation.

THERE ARE MANY IMPORTANT MANUSCRIPTS
THAT ARE READY TO GO TO PRESS, BUT ARE
WAITING FOR A SPONSOR LIKE YOU.

PLEASE CONSIDER ONE OF THESE OPPORTUNITIES
AND MAKE AN EVERLASTING CONTRIBUTION TO
JEWISH SCHOLARSHIP AND CHASIDIC LIFE.

FOR MORE INFORMATION PLEASE CONTACT:

THE CHASIDIC HERITAGE SERIES
770 EASTERN PARKWAY
BROOKLYN, NEW YORK 11213
TEL: **718.774.4000**
E-MAIL: INFO@KEHOTONLINE.COM

COMING SOON!

LECHA DODI 5689 & 5714
By Rabbi Yosef Yitzchak of Lubavitch
and Rabbi Menachem M. Schneerson, the Lubavitcher Rebbe
Translated by Rabbi Ari Sollish

⋘⋙

UMIKNEH RAV 5666
By Rabbi Shalom DovBer of Lubavitch
Translated by Rabbi Yosef Marcus

⋘⋙

TRACT ON PRAYER *Kunteres Hatefillah*
By Rabbi Shalom DovBer of Lubavitch
Translated by Rabbi Y. Eliezer Danzinger

⋘⋙